Alone
among
the
Living

Alone among the Living

G. Richard Hoard

The University of Georgia Press

Athens and London

Published by the University of Georgia Press
Athens, Georgia 30602
© 1994 by G. Richard Hoard

Designed by Betty Palmer McDaniel
Set in 10.5 on 14 Electra
by Tseng Information Systems, Inc.
Printed and bound by Thomson-Shore, Inc.
The paper in this book meets the guidelines
for permanence and durability of the
Committee on Production Guidelines for Book Longevity
of the Council on Library Resources.

Printed in the United States of America
98   97   96   95   94   C   5   4   3   2   1

Library of Congress Cataloging in Publication Data
Hoard, G. Richard.
    Alone among the living / G. Richard Hoard.
        p.   cm.
    ISBN 0–8203–1610–5 (alk. paper)
    1. Murder victims—Family relationships.   2. Bereavement—
Psychological aspects.   I. Title.
HV6515.H59   1994
364.1′523′0973—DC20   93–33746

British Library Cataloging in Publication Data available

Alone
among
the
Living

Chapter One

When I was twenty I came face to face with the old man convicted of paying five thousand dollars for the murder of my father. The old man had been released from prison long enough to have surgery for "the hernias," and during his hospital recuperation I visited him, a pallid man with a swollen belly who sat idly staring at a wall.

It was the only time the old man and I had ever talked. He had come to Jackson's Funeral Home the evening after the murder to offer his condolences and to sign the registration book of family and friends; but I'd not been present to see him, choosing to escape the ritual that follows death, the receiving of visitors who offer their hands and awkward phrases—"if there's anything I can do, let me know"— opting instead to camp out with two friends, drinking four bottles of pop and smoking a cigar to try to purge the taste of death from my mouth. And so until the day I talked to the old man at the hospital, I'd seen him only in the courtroom—except for one afternoon in 1972, five years after his trial and during a brief interval of freedom after an appeal judge in New Orleans had overturned his conviction and released him. During those final days he would ever spend at home, someone drove him past our car, parked between Marlowe's Cafe and the Crawford Long Inn, where my mother and I were set to pull out after having a cup of coffee.

I flinched at my mother's sudden pounding on the steering wheel. "There he goes," she spat, her face contorting with rage.

"There who goes?" I asked, looking over my shoulder at the car now set to pull out onto Jefferson's main street.

"Cliff Park," she said, and as I craned my neck to see him she decried court systems and crooked lawyers and how a person with plenty of money could afford to look long and far enough for a judge willing to make a ruling for the right price.

My mother was right about the courts, I had decided by that time. They seemed more concerned with the rights of criminals than with the rights of victims. Lawyers were considered successful not if they discovered the truth, but if they proved capable of maneuvering back on the streets clients whom they knew were guilty, thus endangering the lives of innocent people. While our family had lost its provider, and my mother had to go to work in a day-care center and sell encyclopedias on the side, justice for the condemned was his own television set, three square meals a day, and visitors. Why, the old man had lost no more freedom than other men his age confined to a nursing home. This was not justice. Wouldn't the only real justice be for the son of the slain to rise up with a gun, introduce himself as the son of Floyd Hoard, and smile at the old man's astonished pleas for his life, relishing his final terror as the pistol was cocked and aimed between his eyes? And should there not be some final terror for the old man, as there must have been for my father, who had known he would die: "He was at my house and he said, 'they're going to get me,'" one of Daddy's friends had said a few days after the funeral. "I had no idea what he meant."

"Put pieces of tape across the hood and if they're broken, you'll know not to get in the car," my Uncle Joe would later tell me he had advised my father. For a while, Joe said, my father had heeded the warning. "Why he quit doing it, I don't know to this day," Joe said. "He just got careless, I reckon."

Or maybe tired of looking over his shoulder every minute, realizing that a life lived in fear wasn't worth living at all, that if somebody determines to kill you, then God Almighty Himself couldn't stop it from happening. Or at least wouldn't. God's only sure-fire way of preventing the lot of us from killing one another was to strike with lightning everybody who'd ever conspired to harm a fellow human. But there wasn't enough lightning in the world to strike all of us who had ever wanted to do someone harm; He might as well send another flood, but that was something He had already tried and determined never again to do. Instead He sent His best work down in His best effort to reform us. But then even Jesus Christ got killed.

Maybe what my father had figured out was that too few people were out to do any real good in the world. It takes someone strong to stand against those who will stop at nothing to protect their own interests. Sometimes a man has to stand alone. And maybe in my father's final thirty seconds of life the groan that was his last was a groan meant to tell my sister, Peggy Jean, and me, who were bending over him and trying to keep the breath of life in him, that in his choosing to defy a corrupt world, in his choosing to "step on one toe too many," as my Aunt Claudine put it, he had set in motion events that led to a death that was as bound to happen as if it had been ordained.

"It has become increasingly difficult to recognize who is directly involved. . . ." Those were his cryptic words found within a week after his death, words penned in a letter written shortly after his election to office as the Piedmont Judicial Circuit's district attorney—solicitor general, as they were called in Georgia back in the 1960s. "It was no concern of ours as long as it did not touch us directly. But now that the finger of guilt has been pointed at us, we realize that the reason we allowed this situation to grow and to remain was because of fear, fear of physical violence or fear of the loss of property.

"We now realize that the preserver of law and order is courage and that fear and inactivity in the face of threats and growing crime can only lead us to moral decay. We now realize, although it is too late to aid the victim, that each inactivity in the face of growing organized crime was a shove toward the murder of our victim, that each time we backed down in the face of threats of violence, we pushed and knocked our victim to the scene where his murder would occur. . . . Please have mercy on us for we will make amends."

My amends for his death would be a bullet between Cliff Park's eyes. That is what I had thought until that day when the old man passed by in the car and the familiar rage welled within me. It was a rage I felt whenever Cliff Park's name was mentioned. Or for that matter, whenever my father was mentioned. But was hating Cliff Park going to help me recover what he had taken from me? Suppose it really had happened as I naively had thought it would happen the day Judge Dunahoo read the sentence of death; that Cliff Park would some day be strapped into the chair and his face covered to hide the eyeballs bulging from their sockets when the volts raced through him, and that I as a member of the victim's family, though only fifteen years old at the time of the trial, would be allowed to witness, and maybe even by some benevolence of the law permitted to throw the switch. Would that electrocution put an end to my hating him? Would it end his dictating to me how I was to feel every day, his killing any chance I had for ever living a life of inner peace? Would I some day die with my fist clenched against God for the pain Cliff Park had caused? No. I was sick and tired of hating. If I ever had the opportunity, I determined that I would visit him, stand up to him as my father had stood up to him, and let him know he couldn't control my life.

My opportunity came the next spring. He'd gone back to prison for a few months, but his health was failing, and when the news came from my older sister, Peggy Jean, who was employed by the hospital, that Cliff Park had had "some kind of hernia operation" and "that he might die," I knew that if I were to see the old man alive this might be my last chance. And as it turned out, it was.

Chapter Two

My father had grown moody the week before his death, "worried," said my mother, who at the time attributed his behavior to a heavy work load; he was to present cases before the Jackson County Grand Jury on the first Monday of August and on top of such preparation was the strain of relocating his law office from the old brick building across the street from the courthouse to the larger frame house on Jefferson's Lee Street. I had seen him rub a furrowed brow on more than one occasion in the past weeks, as if he had a headache, or as if he were lost in thought. His patience was thin; he snapped at my pleas for money or for a game of catch. All I ever wanted was money, he said, and, no, he just didn't have time for baseball.

One thing he always seemed to have time for—at least when no courts were in session or he wasn't pressed by duties as solicitor general to travel to his courthouse offices in the two other county-seat towns of the Piedmont Circuit—was a cup or two of coffee sometime during the morning at Marlowe's Cafe.

About ten o'clock the customary group of men, those not enslaved to clocks, gathered at the cafe to drink coffee, smoke cigarettes, and deliberate on the decline of the world: "It's getting to the point where the average man can't afford to pay his taxes," they would declare, or "President Johnson's wanting him a welfare state at the expense of every decent and respectable tax paying citizen," or "them Russians has got bombs big enough right now to wipe Atlanta off the map," their convictions supported by such phrases as "the paper says," or "I heard on the radio," or "somebody was telling me the other day." Their diatribes and discussions always took place at the two back tables pulled together as one beneath the large wall clock with the sweeping red second hand and near the coffee pot and the watchful eye of Nancy, who seldom saw the bottom of the inside of a cup. For a dime a man could drink all the coffee he wanted, Nancy seeing to it that the cup was full and the cream in plastic containers within reach.

For my father the coffee breaks usually ended after two cups drunk within a half hour. Enthusiastic political discussion might prolong his stay, but only while he stood fishing for a dime in his pocket, extinguishing his cigarette, and all the time saying, "I really need to go."

A cruise past the cafe and a quick surveillance of the cars parked along the curb would reveal who sat inside; my Uncle Albert's white police car, Horace Jackson's green ambulance, which doubled as backup hearse, Runt Moore's blue pickup truck filled with cartons of eggs from his poultry farm, my father's green Ford Galaxy 500, a new 1967 model traded in to replace the old '65. The cars were beside the curb the first day of August when I peddled my bicycle the two miles to town, kicked down its stand on the sidewalk, and opened the glass door to the cafe to feel the welcome shock of cold from the air conditioner. Self-consciously I ambled toward the back table, looking mostly at the tile floor, but glancing up periodically to see the men's amused smiles; amused because in stark contrast to the man who begot me, I had long legs and arms that hung nearly to my knees, and I had my mother's face. And so I waited for the usual remarks: "Gonna be a big man, Fuzzy, if he ever grows into them feet," or "boy's growing faster than a beanstalk; gonna be a six footer for sure," but today no remarks were forthcoming, except from Buck Marlowe, the cafe's proprietor, who sat among his customers. "That's your boy coming back here, isn't it, Fuzzy?"

My father's response was a faint nod and the trace of a smile as he watched my approach. The fingers of his right hand were entwined around the handle of a coffee cup, two fingers of his left hand forming a V, where rested a freshly lit cigarette. Even in the dead of summer he wore his black coat unbuttoned over a white shirt and dark tie, his thick black hair doused with Vitalis and combed straight back. He waited for me to stop beside the table before greeting me, "Hello, son, want some coffee?"

What I really wanted was a nickel for a Pepsi mixed right in the glass at the drug store across the street, but not wishing to insult Buck by refusing his coffee, I politely said, "I reckon."

"Nancy," Buck demanded. "Bring this young man some coffee."

Flushing at Buck's premature bestowal of manhood upon me, I sat down, out of place in shorts and t-shirt among the collars and ties and the adult world of taxes, civics, and politics, none of which aroused any passion within me. My passions were stirred by basketball and teenaged girls, especially one whom I'd actually kissed, or rather had been kissed by, in the Five and Ten Cent Store during the last Christmas holidays, a kiss that had completely caught me off guard; yes, I had been daring Maria Jensen by waving a piece of mistletoe over my head, but I'd never expected her to actually step toward me and plant a quick kiss upon my lips. In reliving the most exciting microsecond in my life, and I had relived it a thousand times, I was appalled to realize that in my astonishment I had actually stepped away from her, never so much as putting my arms about her, much less kissing back. Had I the chance again I would embrace her around her waist, bend her backward in my strong arms (and in the fantasy, my arms were strong), hold her close, her chin and lips turned up toward mine, her eyes closed like those of Scarlett O'Hara, helpless in the arms of Rhett Butler . . .

"You want cream, don't you Dickey?"

"Huh?"

"You want cream?"

"Er, yes ma'am," I replied to Nancy. She removed from her apron pocket two plastic containers and set them beside my cup and saucer. I poured sugar into the coffee, stirring, lifting a spoonful, and with my lips tested the heat of the coffee, with my ears the heat of the conversation, hoping that Runt might break forth with a story: "I had this dream the other night, plumb skeered me to death, worst dream I ever had. I dreamt I was up on Lake Lanier, a campin' out, and it was the middle of the night, pitch black, and I had woke up out on the middle of a sand bar. There wasn't nobody else there but me, and I could hear the water lappin' all around me. . . ."

Or perhaps the talk might drift toward the Braves, who I'd seen lose to the Cardinals in Atlanta the previous Sunday. "That Fuleep Falou is a good player for them Braves," Buck had once said, and I had considered risking impertinence by correcting the pronunciation, but decided only to comment that, "Yes, he's good all right, but he's having an off year. He's capable of hitting three hundred, and his home run production is down, too. I don't think he's recovered from his surgery. . . ." Buck and the other men with him waited politely for me to finish before Buck remarked to my father, "He keeps up with them Braves, don't he, Fuzzy?"

One day, I vowed, I would leave Jefferson and become as famous as Felipe Alou, so that my name, like his, would be spoken with admiration among the men who six or seven years hence would gather at the table: "I heard on the radio the other day that the Braves are trying to trade with Cincinnati for Dickey. Said they'd rather he hit home runs for them for a while rather than against them. I bet he'd love to come back near home to play. He used to love them Braves."

"I saw him play on T.V. last Saturday. He hit a home run his first at bat and next time up he hit a double. Came up the third time and they didn't even pitch to him. Just walked him on purpose."

But today the men's conversation was far removed from anecdotes or baseball. They were talking taxes. "And it's why mine are so high. Now don't get me wrong. I ought to pay my taxes, but when the other fellow doesn't pay his share, and every cent he makes is untaxed profit, then I lose out. I pay my taxes and his taxes, too."

"That's right. It's us tax payers that's getting cheated."

"Well, some folks is doing what they can, I know, but everybody has got to do their part, your judge, your sheriff, everybody."

"But you know, you fine these people and send them back out to their business. Those fines are a drop in the bucket to them. The fines they pay are nothing like the taxes they would pay. You need some jail terms."

"Hell, these people, I'm telling you wouldn't slow down in the damned jail house. They'd have their damned wives operating their business, or their damned children." Voices rose in fervor, but subsided quickly in respect for Buck, who preferred a quiet atmosphere. Nancy, sensing the discussion worthy of another round of coffee, returned with the pot and fresh packets of cream. Cigarette packages emerged from shirt pockets, cigarettes were placed on lower lips to wriggle until fired by matches lit by one flick of the wrist and extinguished by several. Daddy had lit another, a signal that he would stay longer, but he did lift one hand in protest and said, "Half a cup," to Nancy, who paid him no mind and filled his cup anyway. I suppressed a perturbed sigh and let Nancy refill my cup as well, knowing that my trip to the drug store would be delayed at least another ten minutes.

Eternity passed. There were further outbreaks of temper at the disregard for law and order by those who bought and sold "non-tax-paid liquor," a terminology that included beer and wine and any other drink containing alcohol. Jackson County, like the other counties of the Piedmont Judicial Circuit, prohibited sales of alcoholic beverages. Most of North Georgia was "dry," although a few towns, such as Arcade, a village three miles southeast of Jefferson, had legalized the sale of beer and now catered to imbibers from across Northeast Georgia, including students from the University of Georgia, and those high school students old enough to pass for the legal drinking age of eighteen. When the fire of conversation had burned to embers, my father rose abruptly, apologizing that he had to leave, that he really should have left fifteen minutes ago. I followed him to the cash register on the glass counter, where inside lay the Baby Ruths and Butterfingers and the Wrigley's gum, waiting as Daddy fumbled through his pocket for two dimes, which he pitched onto the counter. Nancy took them and pushed buttons on the cash register, its bell ringing and drawer opening and one white sign in the register's window popping up to show "20¢."

After we opened the door to step outside on the hot sidewalk I asked my father for some money. "What do you need money for?"

"I want to go to the drug store and get a drink."

"You just had coffee."

"I know, but I want a Pepsi."

"You could have had a Pepsi at Buck's."

"They taste better at the drug store."

My father said nothing. I pushed no further, staring down at the concrete sidewalk, remembering an ugly incident from the previous week: I had peddled my bicycle to town and stopped for a drink at the drug store. Starting for home, I spotted the passing Galaxy and managed to wave my father down to ask him for a ride home.

"No," he had told me. "I'm in a hurry."

"It won't take you long."

"Son, I don't have time."

"It won't take you five minutes."

"No, you've got your bike. Ride it home."

"But it's too hot. We can put the bike in the trunk."

With a sigh he frowned and said, "Not today. I've got business to attend to."

"Five minutes, Daddy. It won't take you five minutes."

"No, I . . ."

"You can come right back. Come on, Daddy."

"No," he shouted, and failed to fight back the next words, "damn it," before driving off, leaving me stunned; in all my life, I'd never heard him curse.

"Damn it yourself," I had spat toward the back of the car, my eyes welling with tears. What was wrong with him? What work was so important that he couldn't give me five minutes? I vowed that when I turned sixteen and drove around in an air-conditioned car I'd never refuse a ride to anyone peddling a bicycle in ninety-degree heat.

Remembering his outburst and wanting no repeat of such a show of temper, I pushed him no further, staring at the sidewalk. But to my surprise he reached in his pocket and, along with his car keys, removed a nickel. "That's all I've got, son," he said. "That'll buy you a drink, won't it?"

"Yes, sir," I said, taking the money without looking at him. "Thanks."

Without reply he walked to his car, keys jingling as he stepped from the curb. He unlocked the door and sat behind the steering wheel. The ignition key turned. The car cranked and he drove away, leaving me to push the bicycle across the street.

Chapter Three

Sweat had already beaded on my forehead by the time I parked the bicycle near the display windows of the drug store, careful to allow room for passersby on the sidewalk. Before entering, I stooped to pet a hound, which blinked away flies in the shade of the overhang. Grateful for the attention, the dog raised her head, panting, a stream of saliva making a slow journey to blot the sidewalk beneath her chin, her long tail slapping the concrete. "You're a good dog," I said in rising, stepping over the animal, which, as before my intrusion, lay her chin between her front paws.

The store was quiet; except for the few employees, only two women were present, eyeing the knee braces and enema bags beneath the druggist's counter. They were leather-skinned women, one gray and feeble, the other younger but with a face already weathered; country people, the type who, except when sickness brought them to Dr. Adam's office and from there to the drug store, came to town only on Saturdays with their men, who from their pickup trucks sold corn and butterbeans, did business at the bank and maybe at Rosemont's Feed and Seed Store before returning to their homes off the county back roads.

Behind the soda fountain stood Leon, since June an alumnus of Jefferson High School who would soon head off to college, leaving his job of stirring fountain drinks and collecting the potato-chip money of a clientele largely teenaged. Already the air of a collegian was about him; he had a confident smile born of a diploma and the knowledge that for at least another few weeks he had the most enviable job in Jefferson—the power of control over the nozzles and scoops of a popular watering hole for girls. Peak hours for girls came during the school year, when on weekdays shortly after the 3:10 dismissal bell the drug store teemed with laughter and the flirtations of the school's elite, those students who lived in town or owned a car or knew someone else who did and were therefore spared the humiliation of riding the school bus home. Boys strolled in with girlfriends to sit at one of the two booths or on the stools closer to the fountain, freely spending their parents' money on their sweethearts, who batted their eyelashes in appreciation and smiled at the boys whose cocksure curls of the lip said to all onlookers: "Hands off, this girl belongs to me."

"Where is everybody? Man, this town sure is dead," I complained to Leon, slapping my coin on the counter. "Nickel Pepsi."

"Not much happening," Leon agreed, pulling the handle to the Pepsi syrup and adding carbonated water and ice, stirring it in a Coca-Cola glass. "Everything is pretty quiet."

"Too quiet, but at least for you not for long. You'll be a big college man. I bet you can't wait," I said, removing the paper wrap from a straw by tapping one end of the straw on the counter.

"Oh, I don't know. I can't say honestly that I'm looking forward to it."

"Are you crazy, Leon? If I were you I'd be dying to leave. I know I can't wait till I get out of here."

"I used to feel that way, too," Leon replied, holding up a soapy glass to scrutiny by the ceiling light, frowning at what he saw, attacking the glass again with a scrub brush. "But once you get out, it's different."

"Different?"

"Yeah. It's hard to explain, but you'll see when you graduate. It's just a big—change, going off to college and all. I'll miss Jefferson."

"I wouldn't. Not if I was going off to where there were some good looking girls."

"There are plenty of good-looking girls around here."

"Oh, I get it. It's a girl, isn't it? I didn't know you had a girlfriend, Leon. Who is it?"

"No, no, it's nothing like that. It's just that I guess I've learned to appreciate the things I've got around here. Maybe you don't appreciate some things until you know you're about to lose them."

The front door opened. I turned, hoping to spot some lonely blonde with searching eyes hungry for love at first sight. But I groaned, almost audibly upon seeing the football players, two of whom stood at the open door while a third ran the dog from its spot. "Get out of here, y' mutt. Get. I wish I had my shotgun." The two boys at the door laughed at the dog's hurried flight, one firing an imaginary bullet into its flanks before they strutted to the fountain and ordered drinks in a paper cup. "How about it, Hoard?" said Truckie Myers, so nicknamed because he was short but stout, and had surprising ability to flatten linebackers in his path. He wore a sleeveless shirt to reveal strong arms and his deep tan. His haircut looked as though someone had placed a bowl on his head and trimmed everything that showed. With him were the starting center, Benny Durden (who, like Truckie, was a junior, and had been to the same barber, but whose summer worship of the sun and the weight room had cost him blotches across his nose and dead skin peeling from ruddy shoulders), and a tiny offensive guard called Goose, whose vocabulary seemed solely to consist of interjections: "Good gosh" was his favorite, along with "hot'll mighty."

"You've got a lot to do, ain't you, Hoard," said Truckie. "Ain't got time to play football, but you've got plenty of time to sit around in here where it's cool and drink co-colas all day long, ain't you? Say? Ain't you?"

I said nothing, forcing a smile, hoping my face concealed my irritation, for his remark had wounded; three months earlier, after the first day of spring football practice, I had quit the varsity team, heaping shame upon myself from my former teammates and my father. But I had weighed less than 120 pounds last spring when Coach Lofton stuck me at defensive tackle across from boys 50 pounds heavier, one who weighed nearly 200, and those boys had nearly beat me to a pulp. Midway through the practice my head ached so badly that I asked Coach Lofton if I could take some aspirin, and he stared at me as if I'd just asked him to kiss a rattlesnake. Then he did me the big favor of finally allowing me to walk across the practice field to find the medicine kit among the blocking dummies and coolers, and shake two tablets from the plastic jug of aspirin and wash them down with sun-warmed salt water. And then, as soon as I walked back over to the scrimmage to stand behind a few other scrubs, he hollered at me, "Dickey, get back in there at defensive tackle."

I didn't want to play defensive tackle. I wanted to play split end and catch passes. Grimacing, my head still pounding, I had pulled the red helmet over my ears while trotting to the position, my chin strap still dangling as the quarterback barked the signals, "Set. Hit." The tight end came at my chest, the tackle at my knee, and they easily pushed me ten yards downfield. The halfback raced untouched past me. "Come on, Dickey!" Coach Lofton hollered. "Give us more effort than that," and Todd Brown, the tackle, grabbed my helmet and said, "That's pitiful, Dickey. We might as well be blocking the wind." I said nothing because Todd Brown hated me, had one day provoked me into taking a swipe at him by accusing me of having sex with a hag named Lenora Barnes and after he'd asked me for the tenth time if it was good, and had other boys standing around wanting to believe in the fornication, I delivered a swiping blow across his shoulder. He retaliated by shoving me against a concrete wall and slapping my face, leaving me crying tears of rage. "Him go cry. Go cry to your mama," Todd Brown had said. And so, not wishing to provoke him on the field, I silently endured his criticism, and chuckled at his wit.

"You think it's funny, Dickey? You honestly think it's funny?"

"No," I said, "no, I don't."

"Well then how about playing like a man."

On the next play I offered some mild resistance before letting Todd push me down the field.

"Come on, Dickey," Coach Lofton shouted. "Don't let Todd push you around." And that was when I decided that I wouldn't. Never again would Todd Brown push me around, at least not after this practice, for if I survived this day, I determined, I would never step on a football field again.

The next afternoon, instead of going to practice, I went home to lie on my bed and watch "Gilligan's Island" on the black-and-white television in my room, relishing the comfort, wondering why in the world I'd ever wasted my time playing football on the B-team last year, having to practice with the varsity and getting beat up every day when no law said that after spending all day in school I had to spend half the night there as well to play a sport I hated. Why, I was a fool not to have quit long ago.

But my newfound contentment ended that evening when Daddy came home from work. Who had informed on me, I didn't know; Peggy Jean, maybe, or perhaps even Coach Lofton. But whoever had told my father apparently had shown no sympathy toward me, for he was furious: "You mean you just didn't bother to show up?"

"No, sir," I replied, sitting on the floor by the bed, drawing my knees up to my chin, fearing to look at him.

"Why not?"

"I just don't want to play football any more."

"Fine, you don't have to play football."

I sighed in relief.

"But you certainly aren't coming home every afternoon to lie around the house and watch T.V. When you get home tomorrow, I'll have some work lined up for you."

He carried through with his threat, coming home the next afternoon at 3:30, long enough to outline an area beside our house. "I want you to clean out these woods. Pick up these old broken bottles and cans and everything else you see," he said, pointing to the assorted garbage left behind by the previous owner of our house. "Put all this old junk in a pile. Later on I'll let you haul it all off."

"How nice of you," I thought, but knew better than to sass him, at least not within earshot. But after he had driven away I mumbled my summary of such punishment. "He thinks all there is to life is work . . . had babies just to work the fields, too bad my sisters weren't boys so he could get the whole damned woods cleaned out."

The punishment of yard work was inflicted upon me every day for the rest of the week, the labor lasting from the time I arrived home from school until supper. At the end of the week I got Saturday off for good behavior. Mama allowed me an afternoon of freedom in town at Bill Elder's house. Toward dusk I rode my bicycle home and was accosted as I entered the kitchen. "There you are," Mama said, her face red. "I hope you're satisfied at your work. Ask you to clean up the yard and you do your typical halfway job."

"What!" I said, lifting my chin toward her.

"Your father was out cutting the grass where you were supposed to clean up and he ran over some wire and it went up in his leg. Thanks to you, he'll have to have surgery."

I felt as if I'd swallowed a fish bone, but I kept my poise. "Why would he be out there cutting grass when there ain't any grass out there to cut?"

"I wish you could learn how to do something else other than play ball. One of these days you're gonna grow up and see that you've got to accept some responsibility." I had heard this lecture before; Mama wanted to shame me. But I refused to grovel or show remorse, instead walking away through the doorway to my bedroom, locking the door behind me. I cursed my luck. After all that work I had missed one piece of wire, probably a piece of the long cable I'd pulled up from the humus beneath the trees. What were the chances of it ending up in my father's leg? One in a million? Luck or fate or God was clearly against me, I thought, punishing me for not playing football; if I hadn't quit football, I never would have been put to work clearing the woods and the accident never would have happened. I stayed in my room all night, dreading the thought of my father limping in to heap more guilt upon me.

But he never came to my room. He had already been admitted to the hospital in Commerce and by the time I saw him the next afternoon, it was after his surgery. He was in good humor lying in the hospital bed and never hinted that I was to blame for his accident.

Nor did he mention the incident after returning home the next day nor link his surgery with my quitting football. He seemed to have forgot my weakness of not liking a man's sport.

But others like Truckie Myers were not so kind. "You just wait, Hoard," Truckie said, poking my chest with his index finger.

"Wait for what?"

"You wait until cross country season starts. You'll be out there running up and down them hills for about three hours. You'll wish you was back out there with us playing football."

It was one of Coach Lofton's peculiar rules as athletic director and head football coach to punish all basketball players by forcing them to play one of the two autumn sports, football or cross country. And although I knew cross country would be a torture, at least there was no spring practice and no summer spent in the weight room; cross country might be hell for nine weeks, but football was hell for nine months. "I don't think I will," I said to Truckie.

"You just wait, Hoard," Benny Durden sneered. "I can't wait to see you out there puking up your guts."

I grinned in silence until they finally tired of harassing me and walked to stand near the display windows, inserting one penny into the slot of the "Your Weight and Fortune" machine and trying to cheat the scales out of two cents by weighing all three boys from the same coin. "Get on here, Benny. Are you on?

"All right, I'm getting off."

"They like to give you a hard time," Leon said under his breath.

I glanced toward the window to make sure they were paying me no mind before answering, "They don't bother me."

"If you don't want to play football, you just don't want to play."

"And I don't want to play." I said, "You've got to be stupid to work your butt off all year just so you can wear a football jacket. I mean, is knocking heads together and doing grass drills fun?"

"Never could say it appealed much to me. I guess some people must like it."

"Well I don't. So why should I play?"

"Look who's coming!" came Truckie Myers's shout from near the front windows.

"He's coming in here."

Turning toward the front door I saw the object of their attention, T.C. Morrison, dressed in his gray suit and Stetson hat, shuffling through the door opened by the football players. "Come on in here, T.C.," Truckie said, "and let's talk a little football." He followed the old man toward the soda fountain, Benny Durden and Goose behind him, nudging each other in anticipation. "Reckon your football team'll win any games this year, T.C.? If they do, I know I'll be surprised."

T.C.'s football team was Georgia Tech, and because Jefferson was only eighteen miles from Athens and the University of Georgia, T.C. found little sympathy for his team's recent mediocrity. At one time I had been a Tech fan, encouraged by my Uncle Calder, a Tech graduate, and T.C., who years earlier would put a finger beneath the ice cream on my chin and coo to me in my father's lap at Buck's, "this boy's gonna grow up to play football at Georgia Tech." At my nod of agreement, he would laugh raucously and raise his middle and index fingers to say, "Me and you, boy, Georgia Tech." But my father had taken me to some games in recent years at Sanford Stadium, converting me to the Bulldogs, though unlike many of their fans I saw no reason to hate Tech simply because I liked Georgia. If for at least nine games a year, I was for Tech, why trouble T.C. with something he had no need in finding out? I would just as soon told Reverend Ramsey that I didn't believe in God.

By looking in the mirror from the corner of my left eye I could see that T.C. had stopped behind me. He tapped my shoulder. I turned and tried to feign surprise at seeing him.

He glared at me, his eyeballs fidgeting above the pocked nose, his lips clenched. He raised two fingers and with a rasping voice said, "Me and you. Georgia Tech."

I raised two fingers in reply, quickly turning my attention back to the ice in my glass.

"Hey, T.C.," Truckie said. "Don't let Hoard fool you. He ain't for Tech anymore. He's for Georgia."

"Sure I'm for Tech," I said.

"You're a liar, Hoard."

"Don't believe him, T.C. He may be stupid, but he ain't stupid enough to pull for Georgia Tech. He's lying his fool head off."

T.C. turned one of his deaf ears to the boys and reached in his coat pocket, removing his Tech cigarette lighter, holding his cherished icon up for the boys to see as he fumbled through another pocket to find a crumpled cigarette, which he stuck between his lips. He lit the cigarette by cupping his hands as if a stiff wind blew through the room, sucking in quick gasps, emphatically snapping the lighter shut, then raising two fingers before me, saying, "Quick as lightning, busy as bees, Tech'll beat Georgia as much as they please."

"Naw, naw, T.C." Benny Durden howled and Truckie looked toward the ceiling in exasperation at the poem, a staple of any T.C. Morrison diatribe, a poem spoken with the same air of authority with which a Bible thumper would quote the scripture.

"Come on, T.C. Tech ain't gonna beat Georgia this year. They'd be lucky to beat the Georgia College for Women."

"They might could beat the Georgia School for the Blind, but it'd be close."

"They ain't gonna ever beat the Georgia Bulldogs again—ever."

"Ha!" T.C. grunted, and I knew that despite his deafness, which Daddy said grew worse any week after Tech had lost a football game, the boys' taunts had stung T.C. He removed his wallet from a hip pocket and pulled out a crumpled piece of newspaper listing the score of every Tech-Georgia football game, pointing to a place circled in red ink. "Eight long years," he chanted. "Eight long years Tech whipped 'em and nobody thought Georgia would ever win again."

"That was a long time ago, T.C. It doesn't matter any more what happened back then. What happened last year? What's gonna happen this year? That's what counts. We know Tech had a real football team once upon a time, but they don't any more. In fact," he said, winking at Benny, "I heard they were talking about doing away with football out there and just play sissy sports like tennis and basketball." Truckie looked toward me to make sure I'd heard the slander against my sport. "Those boys out there ain't man enough to play football any more. I heard they just sit around all day and drink beer and smoke dope."

T.C. had been pushed enough. He spat out the insult the boys had been hoping all along to hear: "Well, at least Georgia Tech hasn't had a boy marry a nigger girl yet."

The boys exploded with triumphant laughter. T.C. reached in his shirt pocket and turned off his hearing aid before storming out the door. I couldn't help but join the laughter.

"What are you laughing at, Hoard?" Truckie demanded, poking my chest with his finger. "Why didn't you tell him you're for Georgia?"

I said nothing.

"Say! How come?"

"You didn't have the guts to tell him, did you, Hoard? But then you don't have any guts at all, do you? You sure don't have enough guts to play football, I'll tell you that. Why didn't you tell him?"

I couldn't find the words to explain how I was trying to spare a man's feelings. Not to three boys exchanging smirks, ready to pounce on me no matter what my answer. To any one of them, alone, I might have presented my case. Alone, any one of them might have listened. But then, any of them, alone, would have called T.C. "Sir," and left him in peace. But when they were together, they became like a pack of werewolves stalking their prey. Together they combined to become a new, separate personality.

Chapter Four

Across the street from the courthouse was the Westmoreland building, red-bricked and two-storied, the bottom story having two windows originally intended as show windows for a clothing shop but later curtained to give privacy to the patrons of Geneva's Beauty Salon. There were two front doors, the door to the left bearing a white tin sign with black lettering, "Westmoreland and Hoard—Attorneys-at-Law," and opening to a musty stairwell that led to the offices.

My father had occupied those upstairs rooms for fifteen years, nine of them shared with my grandfather, George Westmoreland, the man who had encouraged his son-in-law to quit his job as a teacher and coach, and his summer job as a professional baseball player, to study law. Quitting the classroom I could understand. But baseball? How could anyone quit a career promising fame and applause, especially within a year after hitting better than .350 in the minors? His reasoning, that "You just wake up one day, son, and realize there are more important things in life than playing ball," left me shaking my head in exasperation at the adult mind. Looking back, I think he most likely had decided that he wanted his life to count for something more lasting, that God had put him on the planet to leave some corner of the world in better shape, and whether it was the patch of the woods to be cleaned of bottles and cables and humus, or a nest of bootleggers to be cleaned out from the Piedmont Circuit, he was a man driven toward reformation.

But there had also been a more practical reason for quitting baseball, and had my father put his finger on the whole truth he would have confessed that the financial burden of fathering a second child had forced his decision, for within months of my birth he quit the Phillie's organization and moved his family to Jefferson to share George and Mammie's house and to struggle with an extension course and the bar exam and the initial challenges of building a reputation in a small town.

Within five years his reputation stood firm, thanks to the publicity following the murder trial of James Foster, a handyman painting a house in Jefferson at the time Charlie Drake, a prominent merchant, was gunned down in his own home. Mrs. Drake said she had seen the whole thing, and identified Foster as the killer. All that Horace Wood and my father could do as defense attorneys was file an appeal of the inescapable guilty verdict and hope for a miracle. Fortunately, the miracle arrived when the real killer was tracked down and confessed his crime, saving Foster from the chair. Horace and my father became overnight celebrities, the offices of Westmoreland, Wood (for Horace soon became a partner) and Hoard boomed with business, and Horace wrote a book about the case that practically everyone in Jefferson praised, except my mother, who claimed that the way Horace had written it, "you'd have thought he'd solved the whole damned case by himself."

After a few years the wave of publicity died a natural death, Horace left to open his own office nine miles away in Commerce, and life returned to normal for us, except that two more children, Claudine and Vivian, had been born, and we had moved from my grandparents' home to an old house up the hill from the law office, where we stayed for two years before moving again, this time to a brick house across the street from the high school, my favorite house for I could walk across the street to the practice field and watch the football team or to the paved basketball courts outside the gymnasium, or bike to the drug store or to the houses of several of my friends. It had been a shock to both Peggy Jean and me the spring afternoon my father arrived home early to drive us to the middle of nowhere, almost two miles from the city limits of Jefferson, to show us an old house where he said he wanted to live, a house once white but now bearing only flecks of paint, and with a porch awning leaning precariously, one of its posts having collapsed above the dusty concrete. When I rudely ignored the woman standing in a print dress on the porch and exclaimed, "Good Lord, Daddy, you expect me to live in that," he delivered an elbow to my mouth, apologizing to the woman for both my behavior and his own. The old woman smiled smugly at my humiliation before giving us a tour of the house and the outbuildings. There was a barn no more than ten yards from the back door, a garage covered with sawdust-sprinkled cobwebs, and the final disgrace, an outhouse.

My father had lost his mind, we thought, watching him smile while gazing across the yard at the house as if he saw nothing of the reality facing us, as if he'd come across a castle in the woods. There was nothing to do but to risk further impertinence in hopes of bringing him to his senses. That night I mustered enough courage to approach him.

"Daddy," I said. "Are we going to move out to that old house?"

"Don't you think you'd like it out there where you'd have room to wander around in the woods?"

"I'd rather play baseball."

"You can have you an entire field for baseball and not worry about hitting a ball out in the street."

"But Daddy?" I pleaded. "It ain't even got a bathroom."

He looked at me and frowned. "Is that what's bothering you?"

"Yes, sir, I guess that's the main thing. That and—well, there ain't even a stove to cook on."

He smiled and then broke into a chuckle. "Well, son, you just stop worrying, because we're going to have two bathrooms and a brand new kitchen. It'll be a lot of work for you, but you can do it," he said, teasing me to let me know he was no longer angry.

Within a few months we had moved to the country, after installing two bathrooms and a kitchen with a dishwasher and new cabinets, as well as gas heaters to replace the fireplaces, and new light fixtures. The place no longer looked like a shack but like the house my father had seen all the time, and though I still missed living in town, and never felt as safe in the country as I had with neighbors on all sides, I had grown less embarrassed about such stigmas as riding the second bus home in the afternoons or my father's purchase of goats and pigs, for he also bought a horse, which I rode on the property, and a shotgun, which I used for the liquidation of squirrels, and there was plenty of room for baseball.

After four years it seemed that my father had finally settled in a place of residency, but his wanderlust had driven him to tackle another project, the old house along Lee Street that he and his brother, Joe, converted into law offices. His leaving the old office seemed to me almost like a betrayal of my grandfather, dead for six years, but whose spirit still seemed to live in the back room, where I remembered him smoking cigars in his recliner, thumbing through the newspaper, and chatting with clients waiting to see my father. Most times I could find him at his desk. "Come here, Dickey," he would say, removing a handkerchief from his coat pocket. "Blow." And after finishing the task of making me presentable, he would say, "Now take these two nickels and go down to Brown's and get us two cups of cream," and I would take his money and walk down the alley behind the office to the little store, returning with two yellow containers of ice cream and two wooden spoons, hardly more than flat sticks, and George and I would eat the ice cream in his office. On Saturday mornings, George was always good for at least one dime, enough money for one of my favorite comic books, *Turok, Son of Stone* or *Challengers of the Unknown*.

When not at his desk at work, George usually sat in his chair at home. His one exercise consisted of the three-block walk from home to office each morning, the return trip for lunch, and the repeat performance every afternoon. These efforts left him spent in his recliner, where he watched the news until supper, and afterward returned for a cigar and the evening paper, except during summers, when George and Mammie would sit in rocking chairs on the front screened porch, listening to the crickets and screech owls, the music of someone's laughter drifting from down the hill toward Brown's, or the gears of a car grinding as it turned the corner beyond the Methodist Church. Lying on the porch swing I would fight sleep while watching the lightning bugs and the glow of George's cigarette, its tip fire-red whenever he inhaled the smoke.

For a few years I spent nearly every Friday night with my grandparents. My appearance at the back door was so taken for granted that when I didn't arrive prior to supper Mammie would grow worried and phone our house to ask, "Is my boy coming tonight?" The routine lasted until George's second stroke. After several weeks in the hospital George and Mammie came to live with us in the brick house near the high school. For six weeks they stayed there, George sleeping on a hospital bed in the living room, Mammie in a single bed beside him. As the weeks passed he seemed to grow stronger; he began dressing himself, joining us for meals at the table, watching television in the den, sitting up to read the *Atlanta Journal*.

In November my grandparents returned to their own house but were there only a few weeks before George was back in the hospital. The first Wednesday in December the knock came on the door of my fourth-grade classroom, and my father entered to approach the teacher's desk and whisper something to her. Mrs. Tonge's smile of greeting faded. "Dickey," she said. "Your father wants you to go with him." Beaming, I soaked up my classmate's envy as I gathered my books into one arm, waved goodbye with the other, and followed my father down the long corridor to my sister's fifth-grade classroom. "Peggy Jean's going with us? Daddy, where are we going? Christmas shopping?"

Without reply, he stepped inside Miss Annie's room, returning with my sister, who looked at me with eyebrows raised in suspicion, as if she thought she understood our early departure. "Where are we going, Daddy?" I asked.

"I'll tell you when we get outside, son."

He kept me in suspense until he'd cranked the car and steered it from the parking lot. "You know Mister George was real sick, don't you?"

He waited for my reply of "yessir" before he continued. "And you know he was in a lot of pain for a long time?"

"Yessir."

"Now I want you to know that it didn't hurt him a bit—it was just like he went to sleep—but Mister George passed away this morning."

In the back seat I blinked away tears, my throat swollen with my first taste of real grief. For the rest of the day I suffered through intervals of weeping, sometimes lying quietly before the television, listless, refusing to go out and play. At bedtime, I was still upset and left my room, eyes red from another crying spell. "I can't sleep," I told my father. He put an arm around me and led me into Mama's and his bedroom, where he lay on the bed beside me. "Son," he said, "Mister George wouldn't want you so upset about this."

With my hand I wiped away a tear running beside my nose, wondering how I could not be upset. I would never see George again. Never. Why hadn't anybody told me that George had been sick enough to die?

"You wouldn't want him back to be hurting again, would you?" Daddy asked.

What I wanted to say was, yes, I did want him back hurting again, that it was better to have George hurting than to not have him at all, but I said what I felt I was supposed to say, "No, sir," the words spoken with a yawn of exhaustion, and soon I was asleep with Daddy's arm around me. The next morning he took us to the funeral home, Peggy Jean, three-year-old Claudine, and me, Claudine in his arms, staring down at George's dead and powdered face and pink lips drawn tightly together and his hands at rest on his suit.

"Daddy, that's George," Claudine said.

"Yes, baby, that's George. And that's his new bed. That's where George is going to sleep."

"Sssshhhh," Claudine whispered, index finger going to her lips. "George is asleep."

"Yes, baby, George is asleep."

Six years after George's death his memory still wakened within me at the law office. And the moving of boxes packed with manila folders and envelopes, legal pads, and law books seemed like a betrayal, a desecration of his memory. I grieved, but hid my gloom; Mama would say I was morbid and tell me to "be thankful your father's moving up in the world," a statement typically uttered whenever one of the children complained that Daddy was never home. Never mind that his upward climb was taking its toll. "You just don't know how much pressure he's under right now," Mama had replied to my recent complaint that Daddy never did anything fun with his children. "He's got some big cases coming up. One of them he's hoping will close down the big daddy kingpin. You just cross your fingers that it does."

She had turned and walked away as if harboring a secret. But I knew she was referring to my father's recent efforts to shut down the business of the county's most prosperous bootlegger, Cliff Park. Heck, I thought, I probably know a whole lot more about it than she does. But I would never tell her that. My father had forbidden my discussing what I knew about his activities.

It had been back in early March when Daddy and I were heading toward our cabin at Lake Lanier when we had our first discussion about Cliff Park. We had passed his house with its drawn curtains, the garage with its shut doors, and the yards where sedans and pickup trucks, some with camper tops, were parked, seemingly abandoned, the drivers, I supposed, inside the garage where Cliff was said to keep his inventory. "Well, old Cliff's bootlegging his beer tonight," I said in an effort to make conversation, the remark meant with no more profundity than if I'd said, "All the hoodlums are at the square tonight," or "All the Negroes are at the Happy Hollow Cafe," reports on phenomena I'd witnessed to or heard of all my life. But to my surprise Daddy had taken offense at the remark.

"Now, son, how do you know Mister Park is bootlegging?"

Caught off guard, I stammered out, "I just know."

"How do you just know?"

"Everybody knows. Everybody knows he's the biggest bootlegger in the state."

"But how do you know that?"

I hesitated before replying, cautious lest he trap me into telling too much; a scandal at Jefferson High traced to my tongue could mean bodily harm, not to mention exposure of my own guilt, not that I'd ever bought any beer from Cliff Park or anyone else, but I'd drunk beer a few times and too many people knew it. Carefully I considered my words: "I've just heard some people talking about how they bought beer from him."

"High school students?"

"Yessir."

"Boys your age?"

"No sir, older boys, seniors mostly, saying how they could get beer any time they wanted it."

My father pushed me no further and said nothing more about Cliff Park. At the time I never linked our conversation with the man who visited my father the next afternoon, a Saturday. It was too cold to spend at the water so I had stayed inside the cabin until, growing tired of the enclosing walls, I stepped outside to find Daddy in the front yard talking with a stranger dressed in blue jeans, open-collared shirt, and tennis shoes, not the ordinary attire of most of my father's companions. They abruptly ended their conversation as I approached, Daddy waiting until I reached them before telling me, "Son, I want you to meet Mister Angel."

The man, who had been balancing on a concrete block of the makeshift retaining wall beside the driveway, stepped from the block to offer his hand. "Ronnie Angel," he said, surprising me, for few of Daddy's friends had ever offered me the use of a first name. My father raised his hand to negate the offer. "Mister Angel, son," he said, giving the man a nod sufficient to explain that I had been taught to show respect to my elders. "Mister Angel is with the GBI."

Mr. Angel suppressed a self-conscious grin and held up both hands to wave·off his importance, stepping back up on the concrete block, balancing on one foot. "Does he know?" he asked my father.

"What's that?"

"Does he know what all's going on?"

My father studied me for a few seconds, his face pensive, before saying, "I think he knows more than he sometimes lets on."

I concealed my ignorance with silence, listening for clues that might divulge the mystery of what they thought I knew. But their conversation told me nothing; they spoke of perpetrations and malfeasance and court orders, leaving me bored enough to slip back inside the cabin, but curious enough to later ask Daddy, "What's the GBI?"

"The Georgia Bureau of Investigation."

"Is that sort of like the FBI?"

"Sort of, yes, except that the FBI has the authority of investigation anywhere in the country whereas Mister Angel can only make arrests in Georgia. Do you understand?"

"I think so," I said absently, already pondering my next question, which I hoped Daddy would answer without my having to ask it. But he offered nothing more, and so I asked, "What was Mister Angel doing here? I mean, I've never seen him around before."

"He and I just had a little business to discuss. That's all."

"What business?"

"I'm not real sure it's anything you need to know about right now," my father said. "When I think it's time to let you know, then I'll let you know. Alright?"

"Alright," I said, thinking no more about my father's "business," going about my own until a week or so later when I answered a knock on my bedroom door and found Daddy and Mr. Angel standing before me.

"You remember Mister Angel, don't you, son?"

"Yessir," I said, smiling with pride at my capacity for recall. "He's with the GBI."

"Mister Angel needs your help. He needs to borrow some of your clothes. Why don't you let him look through your closet and your chest of drawers and see if he can find a few things he might can wear."

I wondered if a GBI agent's pay was inadequate for new clothes; Mr. Angel was again dressed in blue jeans and tennis shoes, maybe because he could afford no better, but it wouldn't do to insult or embarrass the man by asking, "Why?" And so I simply told him, "Alright," and led him to the chest of drawers, where he found a pair of blue pin-striped pants, hand-me-downs from my cousin Al, a choice that baffled me. "Mister Angel," I said, as he picked up a white sweatshirt. "I don't mind you borrowing my stuff at all, but Daddy's stuff is—well, it's nicer."

He smiled, undaunted by my question. "I just wanted to get some clothes that a younger man might wear."

I flushed with pride at his classifying me as a young man and watched him pick up another sweat shirt, a blue one with a torn sleeve. "You mind if I borrow this?" he asked.

"No, no, go ahead. But I've got better shirts than that. You're welcome to them."

"No, these will do just fine. Now do you have an extra pair of shoes?"

"Yessir, there in the closet."

He opened the closet door and his gaze fell upon a pair of brown and white saddle oxfords. "What about these?"

I faltered because I wore those shoes to school nearly every day; giving them up meant wearing my dressier shoes, the brown loafers. But cooperating with the law sometimes meant sacrifice, I told myself, and if this GBI agent needed my shoes, whatever the reason, it would be unpatriotic of me to withhold them. "Those'll be fine," I told him. "But if you don't mind, I would like to have 'em back when you're through with 'em."

He laughed aloud and said, "I'll see to it that you get all your clothes back. If you don't get them all back, I'll buy you some new ones, alright?"

"Yessir, but you wouldn't have to do that," I said, relieved that his need for clothing was only temporary, yet puzzled at his remark about buying replacements. If he could afford new clothes for me, could he not have afforded to buy his own?

"I'd better get one more pair of pants if you don't mind."

He draped the clothes over his arm, took the shoes in one hand and said, "I'll get these back to you in about two weeks or so."

"That's fine. No hurry."

Shortly before going to bed that night I heard my father in the kitchen and walked in to find him at the table eating cereal. "Daddy," I asked, sitting beside him. "Why did Mister Angel borrow my clothes?"

He swallowed a mouthful of cereal and said, "Well, son, Mister Angel just wanted to borrow some things that someone a little—a little rougher might wear."

"Why?"

"Is that necessary for you to know?"

"He's wearing my stuff. Why shouldn't I know?"

"Alright," he said, putting down his spoon. "Mister Angel is going to purchase some non-tax-paid beer and whiskey at different places in the next few weeks. Hopefully he'll be able to gather enough evidence to give us some cases in court."

"You mean he's going to raid some bootleggers?"

"No, he won't raid them. He'll just buy some alcoholic beverages, and then if he's able to make enough purchases, there could be some raids later on."

"And he's going to wear my clothes? Sort of like a disguise?"

"I suppose you could put it that way."

My face brightened with pride; wait until my friends heard about this! Me helping the GBI! Why, I was practically an undercover agent myself. But Daddy seemed to read my mind. "Now, son," he said. "You noticed that Mister Angel came here when your mother and sisters were gone. I don't particularly want you to mention this to anyone, not even to them. In fact, I don't care for anyone to know you're even acquainted with Mister Angel."

I nodded my understanding. The work of espionage must be kept secretive. And so not even to my mother did I say anything of what I knew of this probe into the county's underworld. The raid came about a month later, on a Friday night, one night earlier than planned. Mama had answered the telephone shortly after ten o'clock, and to my father's request from the bathtub, "ask if I can call them back," replied that she thought he should take the call now. My father wrapped himself in a towel, dripped water on the carpet in the hallway, and said, "Are you sure?" into the phone before hanging up. Within five minutes he was dressed and gone. My mother walked through the den, where I sat watching television, and said, "Cross your fingers that your Daddy doesn't get hurt."

"Where's he going?"

"He's going out on a raid."

I wasn't worried. My father could take care of himself. I was asleep when he returned home, and when I awoke Saturday morning, he was already gone. The news didn't hit the papers until Sunday morning, when I learned the magnitude of my father's nocturnal activity; more than twenty-one thousand dollars worth of beer and wine had been seized from the home of Cliff Park.

Most of the alcohol was destroyed. Some was taken to the county jail. My father stashed a basket filled with various bottles of beer and wine in our utility room. And when he brought the alcohol to our house he also brought to my room a paper bag with my shoes and neatly folded clothes inside.

Chapter
Five

My father at age forty still led the Jefferson softball league in home runs, hitting his eighteenth and nineteenth for the season on the last night he would ever play the game. "I have to hit 'em out now," he had chuckled modestly a week or two earlier, "so I can trot the bases. I'm getting too old to run 'em any more." He had lost the speed of youth, but he could still run with surprising quickness for his size, short legs pumping beneath the powerful torso, his right foot expertly hitting the bases as he turned each corner without wasted steps. In the field he was able to handle any ball hit sharply near him, but his range had decreased, so that he no longer played shortstop as he had in years past, but first base. "It's my last year of it, I think," he had been overheard saying. "I'm getting too old, and it's hard to find the time."

On that last Thursday evening of his life my father parked his Galaxy outside the gray concrete walls of the softball complex, once the high school football field, now adjacent to the new stadium. I felt a tremor of anticipation that always preceded my competing before the public eye, no matter how small the eye; softball nights drew only a few spectators, wives and children of players, a smattering of girlfriends, and men from other teams hanging around either before or after their own game. The players wore whatever sports attire they could muster: old football jerseys, baseball undershirts with long and colored sleeves, sweat pants, even Bermuda shorts or blue jeans. Only the Lions' Club, with its yellow shirts bearing the club emblem, boasted of anything resembling a uniform.

Daddy had worn his faded yellow shirt on softball nights since I could remember, even back when the league played fast-pitch. Many of the Lions' Club players were holdovers from those days, men in their thirties and forties. They were a team in need of youth, I insisted, boldly offering them my services. "No," Daddy had told me. "You have to be a member of the Lions' Club to play on the team."

"Well, let me join the Lions' Club."

"You're too young."

"How old do you have to be?"

"I'm not sure. But a little older than fourteen anyway."

"Is that the rule?"

"Well, I'm not sure if it's the rule. But it's the rule of thumb. And besides, there aren't any boys your age playing in the league. You might find one or two high school seniors out there, but you just got out of the ninth grade."

"But maybe nobody else my age wants to play. I want to play. Aren't you always saying I shouldn't follow the crowd. Just because my crowd doesn't want to play shouldn't mean I can't."

He shook his head at me, said I might make a lawyer yet, and told me he'd see what he could do. One Thursday in July he arrived home for supper to tell me he'd found a man willing to put me on the roster of a mill team, Standard-Coosa-Thatcher. "Now the man said, and I agree with him, that he's had people out there all season and he couldn't let you just walk out and start playing. But he did say he might could slip you into a game now and then."

I could scarcely settle down long enough to eat supper; I wolfed down my vegetables, changed into a t-shirt and shorts, found my glove and the old shoes with rubber cleats, and waited impatiently as Daddy ate and dressed and finally said, "Alright, let's go."

He drove the two miles to town and the extra mile to the softball diamonds, where a few men had already gathered to field grounders, others warming up their arms by tossing a ball in the outfield or behind the team benches. "Come on over here," Daddy had said, and

I followed him to a bench where a man with a mustache sat writing names in a score book. "This is Mister Brookshire, son. He's the manager of Standard-Coosa-Thatcher's team."

Mr. Brookshire kept his seat, his only stir a tilt of his head to look across his left shoulder and out the corner of his eye toward my father, a movement which, judging by his grimace, must have pained him. He grunted in reply to my greeting, and in muffled tones said to my father something I couldn't quite hear, except for, "Did you explain . . . ," to which my father replied "yes." When they finished talking Mr. Brookshire told me to go to the field and shag flies, so I trotted toward second base, where I stopped to talk with Marcus Anderson, a senior on the varsity basketball team.

"Hoard, what team are you on?"

"Standard-Coosa-Thatcher."

"Me too," he said, pushing his glasses up to the bridge of his nose, suddenly lunging for and fielding a batted ball, then throwing it to the pitcher. "We can use all the help we can get."

"Why? What's your record?"

"We're perfect."

"Undefeated?"

"Ha! I wish."

"You mean you haven't won a game?"

"Exactly. Maybe you're the missing piece to our puzzle."

A grounder came my way. Fielding the ball cleanly, I instinctively looked toward first, and seeing no one covering the bag, feigned a throw and said to Marcus, "Got him by two steps." Waiting for the pitcher to turn and signal for the ball, I asked, "You about ready for cross country?"

"You just made my day bringing up that subject. Hell, no, I'm not ready. I'd as soon be ready for the black plague. I've been running some in the evenings trying to get in shape."

"No kidding? You're running already? Man I haven't done anything."

"I haven't done so much that my tail won't be dragging in front of Coach Keen when practice starts. But I figured I'd better try to do something to get in shape or I'll die. I mean, I'll really die."

Marcus fielded a ball and said, "Here, warm up my arm," and we threw the ball back and forth to one another at the edge of the outfield grass until Mr. Brookshire called us to the bench and read the lineup. Even though I had known I would be a substitute, I still felt a wave of disappointment at not hearing my name read. Except for two trips to the water faucet, I sat on the bench until the game ended, watching my new team get pummeled by more than ten runs. Come Monday I sat watching again. By the third inning the game was out of reach. I reasoned that surely he would put me in the lineup. But the innings passed, and no call came, and after the game ended with me still on the bench I decided that my joining this team had been a mistake. Thursday when Daddy said it was time to leave for our games, I told him, "I think I'll stay home tonight."

"No, you won't, either. Now get your glove and shoes and let's go."

"Why? I won't get to play."

"You've only been twice, son. You're not quitting after I made the effort to get you on the team. You've got to learn to be patient. Keep showing up and pulling for the team, and you'll get your chance. You can't just quit something when it doesn't go your way. You'll end up quitting everything, like you quit football."

I winced. So he was still ashamed of me for hating a real man's sport. Sullenly, I shuffled to my room to change shirts and get my glove and shoes for another evening of warming the bench. "Yeah, Daddy, yeah," I thought as the innings passed. "Just keep showing up and I'll get my chance. Sure. You don't know everything." If there was a lesson he wanted me to learn, I reasoned, I had already learned it. I would never again pester him to help me join any more teams.

The next Monday I suffered again through the first six innings of another defeat until finally Mr. Brookshire gave me a chance. I trotted toward right field, doubtful that any of our opponent's right-handed batters would hit a ball toward me. But I was wrong. The second batter tested me, hitting a fly ball that stayed up long enough for me to catch. The next batter hit a clean line drive toward me, but stayed at first base when I fielded the ball on one hop and made a strong throw to second. The game ended before anyone else hit a ball my way, and so I left the field supposing that I had played about as well as I could. Apparently Mr. Brookshire thought so, too; at our next game he called out my name as the starting right fielder. A week later (the first Thursday in August) when Daddy and I passed through the gate, he moved me to left field, where more balls would be put into play.

To the surprise of our opponents, and maybe to our own as well, we struck for a big inning early in the game, and, for the first time all season, entered the final inning with a lead. With two out, runners on second and third, and the tying run at the plate, the batter lofted a high fly down the left field line. "It's foul! It's foul!" someone from the infield shouted, but I was already racing toward the foul line, never letting up my stride nor taking my gaze from the ball, hearing someone's remark from the bleachers that "He's going after it, ain't he?" crossing the line, reaching across my body and toward the ground, feeling the ball stick in the webbing of my glove.

"He caught that ball!"

"He sure did!"

The game was over. Our first victory. I heard some applause from the few people behind the bench as I jogged toward the infield. My teammates shook my hand and patted my back. Marcus grabbed my arm and said, "Great catch, Hoard."

Basking in the attention, I glanced behind our bench where stood a cluster of men, some wearing the yellow shirts of the Lions' Club, among them my father, holding his glove. What did he think of the catch? Someone had grabbed his shoulder and was talking to him. Had he missed it? I watched him until I caught his eye and saw crossing his face the faint trace of a smile.

At the time I had no idea of the profundity of the moment, his smile of amazement that I could pull off a play to rival one of his own, a smile that I would later cling to as his blessing of approval. Looking back, I now realize that every acrobatic catch, every basket in the clutch, and certainly the touchdown-saving tackle I would later make, was a desperate effort to reclaim that blessing.

Chapter
Six

Sunday mornings held a certain peace about them. It was the Lord's Day, not to be profaned with unnecessary labor, but kept hallowed by rest; an extra hour or two of sleep, another hour or so of my baseball game played with cards and dice, perhaps some good reading (until the afternoon, when the church programs on television had ended and the movies and sporting events had begun), maybe even the restful activity of fielding baseballs with a friend.

Hours after sunrise on August 6, blue jays shrieked outside my open windows, waking me, or had I been awakened by another sound, a distant voice calling my name? No, it was only a dream, I decided, reaching to pull the sheet over my shoulders before drifting again toward sleep.

"Dickey." There it was again, the voice, my mother's voice now closer to my room. "Get up now. Get ready for Sunday School and church."

Our church was the Methodist Church, a stone building on a corner lot across the street from my grandmother's house. At this church's sanctuary I'd been baptized as an infant, confirmed as a fourth grader, and bored by countless sermons since my life began. As the years had passed, I wrestled with maintaining righteous behavior for those two hour stretches by napping, coloring pictures from the Sunday School lesson, doodling on bulletins, memorizing the Apostles' Creed, enjoying a romantic fantasy while staring at a young woman in the choir—always breathing a sigh of relief when the penance of Sunday morning had ended and I could remove the coat and necktie and stoop to being myself.

Sunday mornings in church stirred within me not memories of hope and grace, but of judgment. My first spanking there, at least the first I could remember, had come when as a four year old I was inspired to stand in the aisle and sing my rendition of "Hound Dog," an act cut short when Daddy leaped up to usher me down the aisle between red-faced and quivering adults who looked at me, though they pretended to gaze straight at the preacher, who had never missed a word of his sermon despite the distraction. Once outside the front door my father removed his belt and halfheartedly swatted me across my legs. I howled in rage. The previous night he had requested a repeat of my Elvis impression before the next-door neighbors. In church the same behavior was frowned upon. Now I realize the spanking had been as much of a performance as my song, something he did against his will for the benefit of others judging his response to my misbehavior. It was my first brush with the brutal world of church politics. He led me back to my seat as I sniffed back tears and sat quietly for an eternal five minutes before yielding to the distraction of Billy Lee, who tried to cheer me up by sticking out his tongue at me. Mama picked me up and set me down between Peggy Jean and her, and when I turned my head to watch Billy some more, she pinched me.

I hated church. Through the years I endured reprimands, threats, and punishments for talking during the sermon, or giggling, or cracking knuckles, or unwrapping candy, or passing notes or bubble gum or gas (it was Clarence Wilson's explosion during a "moment of silence" that had turned faces of horrified adults toward us, costing me a lecture at home for something completely out of my control) or writing a four-letter word on the chalk board, or proving my courage between the Sunday School hour and worship by climbing thirty feet into the highest limbs of a cedar tree, terrifying the adults who shook their heads and declared that at the next board meeting they'd see that something was done about that tree. But apparently the board decided that the tree would stand, for wasn't the real issue parents who failed to control their children? Tell the parents to keep their children on the ground. And so we were ordered, with threats, and for one Sunday, or maybe two, we obeyed until the issue had passed and nobody bothered to stand guard over us any longer, at which point the children continued their ascents toward heaven whenever they knew adult eyes were turned away.

One evening when the trusting adults had left the fourth graders unsupervised after the Methodist Youth Fellowship, Billy Lee climbed into the branches of the cedar and plucked two green cones, as heavy and solid as baseballs, dropping them to the ground, then swinging down himself to retrieve them. "Bet you I can hit Miz Davis's window from here," he said, brandishing the cones.

From where he stood, it was a long throw. "Aw," I scoffed. "There's no way."

Billy carried the cones closer to Martin Street, standing nearly at the bank above the sidewalk. "Hey, wait!" I protested. "Anybody could hit it from there." Paying me no mind, Billy hurled the first cone, which blasted loudly against a wooden shutter. "No, Billy, don't!" I pleaded. "You can do it. I know you can do it."

The second cone shattered a window pane and landed somewhere in the room where Colonel and Mrs. Davis were watching television. An unseen hand parted the curtain. Mrs. Davis's white hair appeared, then her pale face. I clutched at Billy who had fallen in triumph on the lawn and lay kicking the air and giggling. "Get up," I screamed. "Run." But it was too late. Mrs. Davis had already waddled to the front door.

"Ah see you, Billy Lee. Ah see you, Dickey! Y'all didn't think ah was home, did you? Well, ah'm gonna tell y'all's mamas on y'all."

She must have gone immediately to her telephone for when I arrived at home Mama already held the fly swatter made from window screen. "Mama, I didn't do it," I protested at the first swat across my legs. "Mama, I swear I didn't. I was trying to stop Billy. I swear on the Bible. Ask Jim. He'll tell you."

After another few swats, Mama acquitted me with a warning that I was never to play with Billy Lee again, a reprimand often given and as often forgot within a week.

In fact it was within a few weeks of the pine cone incident that Billy, visiting his grandmother, Miss Richie, who lived across the street from my own grandmother, and I found ourselves playing together after school. We had roamed the churchyard, climbing the cedar for a while, picking cherry plums and throwing them at one another in battle, climbing over the cast-iron fence of the churchyard's one solitary grave, William Duncan Martin's, who'd bequeathed money to the church in exchange for a final resting place beneath a large headstone bearing the words:

"Remember, man, as you walk by,
As you are now, so once was I.
As I am now, so you shall be.
Prepare for death and follow me."

Reading the poem I shuddered and said, "Let's get out of here, Billy."

"Why?"

"There's a dead man under there."

"Really?"

Billy took a notion to dig up the grave and look at the man's bones and when I said I wouldn't help him, he taunted me. "Chicken. Brawk, brawk, brawk. Chicken."

"I ain't."

"You're chicken if you don't help me dig up these bones."

We used a stick and a spoon retrieved from his grandmother's barn door, digging a hole a foot or so deep until finally, the stick met an unyielding stratum. "It's a rock," Billy said.

"No, it's his coffin," I said. The image of a corpse reposing barely a foot or two away suddenly sent a chill down my spine. "Come on, Billy," I said. "Let's quit. We've gone deep enough."

"No," Billy said, laughing wildly. "I'm gonna dig him up."

"Come on, I think this is against the law."

"Noooo," he groaned, and apparently enjoying the sound of the word, he tilted his head back and groaned like a wolf. "Noooo. Noooooooo. I'm going to dig him up."

A wrestling match ensued, Billy laughing the whole time I was struggling against him to fill up the hole, until finally he lay spent by his laughter. I threw dirt in the hole, oblivious to whomever it was who passed by in a car and informed. My mother accosted me the minute I entered the house, "Why were you digging in the churchyard?"

"I don't know. Billy wanted to dig."

"If Billy Lee stuck his head in the fire, would you do it, too?" she asked me.

"No, ma'am."

"Mark my words, and I don't mean maybe, I don't ever want you playing with Billy Lee again."

But it was impossible for me to never play with Billy Lee again. As long as Mama insisted that I attend church, she could hardly prevent the influence of its participants. And the participants, without such deterrents as cuts in conduct grades or added homework or the paddle to ward off mischief, were out of control, pulling hair and slapping the backs of heads and singing with Italian accents, "He died on-a the cross to save us from-a sin. Everybody ought to love-a Jesus." The poor woman who taught our class, apparently trying to practice the fad theology that she preached (that Jesus came to earth to be our example, forgetting that he called the scribes and Pharisees a bunch of hypocrites, remembering only that he was courteous to dumb sheep and to children, thinking that gentle Jesus, meek and mild, as wore a smile on his face the whole time he was cleaning out the temple) maintained her hypocritical smile while reprimanding us: "Let's try to be like Jesus, boys and girls. Remember we're in the church. God is watching us." It was hard for us to take seriously anyone smiling. An honest reprimand should have been accompanied by a threat and a stern gaze. But we soon learned not to trust her. By the time I was in the car my parents already knew of my sins and were threatening the rod of affliction.

The passing years had brought a further distaste for the weekly homage paid to dead characters of an ancient world; homage to Jesus, who from the portraits of him in the Sunday School assembly room looked like a woman with a beard, with praying hands as soft as his eyes, and drooping shoulders, crucified in his day, no doubt, for the same reasons a sissy today would get beat up for preferring hopscotch over football. And when he was nailed to the cross, he looked down on the bullies and smiling sweetly said, "Father, forgive them, for they know not what they do," when anybody I'd ever met or wanted to be like would have tossed hand grenades to save his own skin. "Jesus is our example," said the Sunday School teacher. And yet, who could possibly have wanted to be like him?

"Get up now," my mother called again. "And I don't mean maybe." I groaned from my bed. "Why do we have to go up there?"

"Because."

"Because why?"

"Because I said so."

"Why do you say so?"

"You need to go. All of us need to go. Maybe it'll improve your attitude."

"I don't get nothing out of going up there."

"Well you receive what you put into it," she replied smugly, as if she'd uttered something profound. "Now I don't want to hear any more of your lip."

Climbing from the top bunk, I put on some pants and staggered into the kitchen to sit at the table and stare blankly before me until Mama's hand appeared with the coffee pot, and she poured the arc of black liquid into a plastic cup. Eyes half closed, I spooned out some sugar and sprinkled it into the coffee, added milk from a carton, more sugar, more milk, stirring the brew. After a sip or two from the spoon, I picked up a fork and cut into a fried egg, its yoke flowing like a tiny river along the banks of a strip of bacon.

"I see I'll have to get you up at eight o'clock next Sunday," Mama fussed.

"Yeah, you do that," I retorted, knowing full well that the next day I would leave for my cousins' house for two weeks of playing checkers with my Uncle Calder at his store or playing baseball with Ricky Lister and the sons of black pulpwooders, drinking Nehi Grape, eating watermelon, sometimes merely lying around and daydreaming, far from my mother's demands and my older sister's arrogance, which was inflated by the prospect of getting her driver's license, since she was assuming that once she and Mama had delivered me to the bus terminal in Athens on Monday she could take the driver's exam. "Now we'll have a ride home from school!" I had exclaimed the previous week on her sixteenth birthday, my way of offering congratulations.

"No, you won't either. You can ride to school with me in the mornings, but you'll have to take the bus home in the afternoons."

"Take the bus home! You're as crazy as you look!"

"I'm not carrying y'all around with me after school. I've got things to do."

"What things?"

"Things that are none of your business."

"Yeah, like sit in the drug store and flirt with the boys. Well, it won't do you any good. Won't none of 'em have you, you fat pig."

"You make me sick," she hissed, her face turning crimson. "You make everybody sick, you little ass. You don't have any friends."

"That's right. Because you're my sister."

"Oooh, you make me puke. I wish you were dead."

"Aw, go to hell."

"Ass. . ."

Give her two weeks of driving around by herself and then we'd bring the subject up again, I told myself, slowly eating my fried egg. In the meantime I didn't care what she did. I'd be down at Calder's and not have to watch her act like the Queen of Sheba. At Calder's my only reminders of home would be the presence of my two little sisters who were already there, but I would be subjected to them only at night.

"Hurry up, now," Mama called from somewhere in the front of the house. "Peggy Jean and your daddy's already left for Sunday School." I kept my seat. Every minute wasted here was a minute I wouldn't have to spend in church. And so I finished my coffee before rising to swagger into my room and find a white shirt, which I put on in the pretense of getting ready, returning to the kitchen to pour another cup of coffee. By the time I had managed to put on socks and shoes and to clip on my necktie it was after ten o'clock. And by the time Mama had driven us into town we were fifteen minutes late.

She parked her blue station wagon in my grandmother's driveway and while walking toward Mammie's door told me to go to Sunday School. Spitting in disgust on the asphalt, I sauntered across the street and turned the corner of the church building, passing beneath the open windows of the room where the children sang in assembly, "He died on the cross to save us from sin, everybody ought to love Jesus," sung now without Italian accents, baby stuff, I thought to myself, like the whole lot of church crap. Why did anybody bother to mess with religion, anyway? I'd never seen anybody act like they really enjoyed it. But if you didn't attend church, people would think you were evil, and what people thought mattered. As long as it was the right type of people.

"The little yellow bird sings a very sweet" sang the children. "I can't take this," I mumbled with a profanity, glancing around the yard. No one had seen me. Turning, I headed back toward Mammie's house and entered the back door.

"I thought I told you to go to Sunday School," my mother cried.

"You expect me to go in there twenty minutes late?" I retorted, glaring at her as if our tardiness were her fault. Picking up the newspaper I found the sports page and hoped that Mama and Mammie would lose themselves in conversation and let the hour slip away.

"No," Mammie was saying loudly, as if Mama were in the next room instead of at the table beside her. "I just hadn't even got out of my gown this morning. I know I should have got on up and got ready for church."

"Dickey just dragged around or I would have made it myself," Mama said, pouring herself a cup of coffee. I involved myself in an article about the Atlanta Braves, paying scarce attention to them until Mammie said, "Richie says that Horace has a body over there."

Miss Richie, along with Mammie, attended practically every funeral in town, either because they knew the deceased or knew somebody kin to the deceased or knew somebody who was a friend of somebody kin to the deceased. And so whenever the embalming room lights came on at Horace's funeral home the phones began ringing, "Who was it . . . Miss Hood might know . . . called her and she said . . . his sister is that Miz Linton . . . don't know her myself . . . funeral is at two . . ."

"Who died?" asked my mother.

"Richie says it was Tommy Winters."

"No," my mother wailed. "I didn't know Tommy Winters died."

"Yeah, he died yesterday. Richie said he just dropped over with a heart attack." Mammie described death in the same tones she used to describe insanity ("just walking down the street and went crazy)" as if death and insanity were like a sudden loss of bowel control, a shameful embarrassment.

Setting down the newspaper, I asked Mammie, "Who's Tommy Winters?"

My ignorance offended her. She seemed convinced that Tommy Winters and I were best of friends. "You know Tommy Winters. He works down at the shoe shop."

"The man with black hair?" I asked.

"No," Mammie scolded. "You know Tommy Winters. You'd always see him standing back around the shoe shine stand. He was bald headed."

"He would always speak to you whenever you came in," Mama added.

"No," I said, looking at the ceiling. "I don't know him."

"Yes, you do."

Weary with the argument I picked up the sports section again and waited on them to quit scolding me. "You know Dickey knows Tommy Winters."

"He doesn't pay any attention to what's going on around him. It's time he learned to pay attention to something other than ball."

"Oh, he'd know Tommy Winters if he saw him."

"Say," my mother said. "I wonder if Horace would let me see him."

"I don't know, Imogene. I guess you could go over there and ask. If there isn't any family over there, you might can."

"He'd probably let me," Mama said, heading for the door, telling me over her shoulder, "You go on to church."

Chapter Seven

I suppose there is ammunition for the doctrine of total depravity when one considers that in choosing between listening to the word of life from a living preacher or looking at a corpse in a casket, I chose the corpse. Maybe it was because looking at the corpse would make me feel the adrenaline of fear that let me know that I was alive. The boredom of worship made me feel nothing at all, and therefore dead. Besides, if a glance at Tommy Winters was important enough for my mother to skip worship, then I supposed I needed to pay my respects as well. Setting down the newspaper, I stood to leave.

"Are you going on over to the church?"

"In a minute I am," I said, stepping outside and turning toward the backyard and the collapsing wire fence that separated Mammie's property from the grounds of Jackson Funeral Home. Crouching from behind a stone retaining wall, I watched Mama, who had driven up Martin Street and turned the corner to park in the front yard, walk to the door. Once she'd gone inside, I climbed the concrete steps leading up to the railed porch and opened the front door in time to catch Mama's sharp glance before she descended the stairs to the embalming room. I followed, glancing at my watch before entering. Nearly eleven o'clock. The worship hour.

On a cot beside a blue casket lay a bald man dressed in a navy blue suit. My cousin Al, Albert's son, who worked part time for Horace, stood beside the casket, acknowledging me with a nod before helping

Horace lift the sheet on the cot and slide the body into the casket. The corpse's nose quivered like gelatin until the vibrations ceased and the nose settled into its eternal posture. I studied the dead face, but for the life of me I couldn't remember ever seeing Tommy Winters. "He looks so good, Horace," my mother said. "Just so natural."

Horace thanked her and after arranging the hands of the corpse to rest on its thighs, closed the lower portion of the casket's lid. I noticed that Tommy Winters would be buried without his shoes. It made sense, I reasoned, for how else could a specter sneak up behind anyone during the night?

"Want to help me?" Al asked after the casket was closed.

"Yeah," I said, bravely grabbing a brass handle to the casket. We pushed the cart toward the elevator, where Al pressed the button to the door and stepped from behind the casket to push it into the chamber. He stepped back outside. "We're not riding?" I asked.

"No," Al replied tersely. We walked upstairs to the elevator door and pushed the button, the motor grinding until the door opened and Al pulled the casket out into the hallway. It occurred to me to ask why we hadn't ridden the elevator, but I decided to keep silent. Maybe Al didn't want to be closed up in a chamber with a corpse any more than I did. Suppose Tommy Winters rebelled against death and started beating on the casket lid? But I was being silly, I told myself. As Mama often said, "You don't have to be afraid of dead people. It's the live ones you have to worry about. Nobody's ever come back from the dead."

"What about Jesus?" I had once asked her.

"That's different."

"How?"

"Don't be so morbid. When you're dead, you're dead."

Tommy Winters was dead. Which was easy to believe with Al standing next to me at 11:20 on a bright Sunday morning, and with Horace and Mama in the next room. But later that afternoon when Peggy Jean and Mama had left home to help Daddy move boxes from his office, I felt an uncanny presence with me, even in broad daylight. My shaking of the dice and their falling on the cardboard playing field were the only sounds I heard until there came the creak in the hallway. A settling of the house?

Holding my breath, I strained to listen. Even the birds were deathly silent. Had something taken a step out near the telephone in the hallway? My heart seemed to pound in my chest. A chill raced down my back. I stared at the door expecting the shoeless corpse in the blue suit to suddenly glide into the room with mouth frozen in a leer, eyes open and sightless, nose quivering, stiff finger pointing at me. I would just drop over dead, white haired with my own eyes open in a final gaze of horror. For several minutes I sat and stared before finally picking up the dice and rattling them again, and while I rattled them, a noise from the hallway broke the silence. I gasped. The telephone. In the hallway. What if the ghost were still there? I scolded myself. The middle of the afternoon, and here I was scared of ghosts. I leaped up and ran toward the hallway, picking up the telephone.

"Hello, Fat Boy. Want to go to a movie tonight?"

I breathed easier. Daddy's older brother, Joe, who sporadically appeared in Jefferson to stay for months at a time, helping my father with building projects—the house we had moved to in the country, the lake cabin, an old house in town purchased and made into a boarding house, chicken houses, the new law office on Lee Street—only to disappear in a fit of wanderlust that might last for months or years. His most recent stay had been his longest, more than a year, much of it spent at our house, where he had shared my room.

His first week there had created some tension; I wanted overnight company for Friday, but here was a grown man sleeping in my room. Mama's response to my complaint was, "Don't let me even hear you say the word 'company,' and for goodness sakes don't let Joe hear you complain. How do you think he'd feel if he thought he was in your way?" And so I had moped around for more than a week, angry at this intrusion into my life, until the approach of Joe's second Friday with us when it had become apparent that he intended to stay indefinitely, and I risked hurting his feelings by timidly asking him what he thought about my having overnight company.

Joe glanced about the room, nodding as if deep in thought, finally breaking a long and uncomfortable silence by asking, "How many beds we got in this room?"

There was my top bunk, Joe's lower one, and the double bed beside the opposite wall. "Three," I replied.

"Well, I don't know about you, but I ain't planning on sleeping but in one of them. Unless you plan on sleeping in more than one bed, it looks to me like we've got plenty of room."

"You mean you don't care?"

"Shoot no. Y'all ain't gonna bother me none, and I sure as heck ain't gonna bother y'all. About the only time I'll ever be around is when I come in to go to bed, and if your friend don't mind my snoring, then I don't see any problem."

And so for Friday night I invited company, Bill Elder, who came despite his initial misgivings about sharing a room with an adult. His anxieties quickly faded (as did the anxieties of all my friends) upon perceiving that Joe was no threat, for Joe stayed in town until late and when he did come home he went straight to bed and fell asleep with amazing rapidity, snoring through television shows or radio music or drowsy conversations about girls. Joe's presence was no more threatening than that of a sleeping hound. He came and went as he pleased, as he'd always come and gone as he pleased during his life. He made few demands on me, never griped about the lamp bothering him when I read late at night, never told me when to go to bed or when to do my homework, never ridiculed my language or my logic, never bossed me, never treated me like a child, and as long as I proved able to keep a secret, he allowed me to drive the pickup truck on paved roads, smuggled to my room late-night milk shakes from the Humdinger Drive-In, and handed me a quarter without question when I told him I really needed one. In return I tried not to complain when he asked me to fetch nails or stir paint or hold up sheetrock while he stapled it to a wall.

For more than a year we shared the room until, without explanation, Joe moved to the boarding house, his exit as sudden as his entry. I missed his presence on the lower bunk, for as long as Joe had snored beneath me I had no fear of the dark or the dead people I'd seen. Since his departure, the phobia had been rekindled, and I had resorted to going to bed before the rest of the family so as to be asleep before all the lights were out. Or I would keep on my lamp and sleep with a book on my pillow, avoiding ridicule by pretending to have fallen asleep while reading. I was always relieved on the few occasions Joe returned for a night or two, but most of the time he slept at the boarding house in town.

"What's playing? Not that it matters. I'd like to go see anything."

"Some war movie. The Dirty Dozen.

"I reckon I can. I'll have to ask. Mama isn't—no, she's coming up the driveway now."

And so that night Joe and I went to see the movie about some prisoners trained for a special mission in Germany, where most of them were slaughtered. After the movie we stopped by the Varsity Drive-In where Joe bought us both a Coke to drink on the way home. By the time we reached the Brockton Road, which passed by our house, I was sucking the final drops of the Coke through the straw.

"The soda fountain blues," Joe said.

"What's that?"

"The soda fountain blues? That's when you've finished up your drink but you wish you had a few swallows more."

"Oh, I understand."

We lapsed into a comfortable silence, me nibbling at the crushed ice from my cup, Joe removing a pack of cigarettes from his shirt pocket, tapping the box with one finger so that a cigarette emerged, grabbing the cigarette between his teeth, and pushing in the truck's lighter. Our silence was finally broken by my question prompted by thoughts of the movie: "Joe, were you ever in a war?"

"Yeah, Dickey, I was."

"What war?"

"World War II."

The lighter ejected and Joe reached for it, lifted it to the cigarette, inhaled deeply.

"What were you in? I mean the Navy? The Army? Or what?"

"I was in the Merchant Marine," he replied, offering no further explanation.

"What's the Merchant Marine?"

"Someone has to carry supplies and materials for the men doing the fighting, see that they get their food and ammunition. We'd ship materials to different places."

"Did you ever have to kill anybody?"

"No," he said, pausing to take another draw from the cigarette. "I didn't. Well, I nearly did one time."

"Really? How come?"

"Well, we was out there on this ship, and had been out there for about six months without ever seeing land, and there was this nigra cook—now, mind you, I ain't got a thing in the world against a colored man; you know, if he treats me decent, then I'll treat him decent, too. But this fellow, he couldn't read a lick, and every day he'd come down to where I was and say, 'I forgot my glasses, would you read the menu to me?' and I'd read him the menu, and sure enough, he'd memorize it to a tee and he'd cook everything I told him to, but if I didn't read it to him, he wouldn't know what to cook."

He paused to take another draw from the cigarette and to flick ashes out the window.

"How'd you know the man couldn't read, Joe?"

"Well, I knew he couldn't be forgetting his glasses every day, and so one day I told him to go get his glasses, that I was tired of having to read the menu to him every day, and he said something about how he had lost his glasses, and I told him he wasn't fooling me none, I knew he couldn't read, and he'd be better off just telling me the truth than coming down there every day acting like he forgot his glasses."

"What happened?"

"He didn't like me telling him that. And after a while, things just started building up between us. Mind you now, it took over six months for it to build up, but one day he came at me with a knife and I swung at him with a fire axe."

"Would you have killed him?"

"You're danged right I would have killed him. There comes a

time, Dickey, when you've got no choice but to kill a man. Now granted, you've got to look for other ways to solve a problem first, but if you can't find any other way, then you've got no choice but to kill a man."

"What ever happened? Did you ever fight again?"

"No, but I tell you I was sleeping with a knife under my pillow for a week because I thought that crazy idiot was liable to come in my room and try to cut my throat."

"Because you found out he couldn't read? Man, he really was crazy, wasn't he?"

"You're danged right he was crazy. And crazy people will kill you. There are some people you've just got to watch out for."

Joe turned the truck onto our driveway and drove up toward the house and the front yard illuminated by a street light on a utility pole. He stopped the truck beside Daddy's car, keeping the motor running, a signal that he would leave once I'd got inside.

The porch light came on and the front door opened. Daddy stepped outside, shielding his eyes from the glare of the headlights with one hand, pulling his white t-shirt down around his white boxer shorts with the other. He said, "Did you enjoy the show, son?"

"Yes," I replied, glancing up at him. Maybe it was the glare of the lights, causing him to squint and thereby curl his mouth up into a smile. But, no, his entire demeanor had changed; he showed no signs of tension, considering the cases he was presenting to the grand jury the next morning. He wore the serene look of a man who'd already heard the judge rule in his favor.

In my bedroom I put on some pajama shorts and a t-shirt and climbed into the top bunk and turned out the light, staring into the blackness of the kitchen, listening for those familiar sounds that would disclose whether Daddy had decided to watch television or go to bed. All was quiet. He had gone directly to bed. My mind flitted between the black cook on Joe's ship and the prisoners of war in the movie—and death. Tommy Winters. No, I told myself, don't think about him. But I couldn't help but think about the bald and shoeless man rising from his blue casket, dead eyes fixed in a lifeless stare, dead brain fixed upon revenge toward those he'd spoken to all his life but who had failed to notice him. Silently he glided down the Brockton Road, turning through the woods near our house. Even now the dogs barked at him whose finger pointed at me, beckoning me to follow him to the realm of shoeless dead. In the kitchen the floor creaked. Trembling, eyes wide with terror, I fumbled to turn on the lamp, got out of bed and found a book, returned to lie between the sheets, holding the book, staring into the kitchen, listening to the dogs that knew of unseen danger lurking in the yard.

Chapter Eight

Unseen footsteps entered my room. An unseen hand turned off the lamp, waking me. It was morning. Through closed eyelids I sensed daylight, but lay motionless and drifted again toward sleep. Another hour or two would pass before Mama would wake me to go to Athens and from there to Calder's and the peace that would come with two weeks away from home. Most likely she would scold me for leaving on the lamp, but in another two hours maybe she would have forgotten. I drifted again toward sleep, but was suddenly jolted by—a thunderclap? Someone shooting to scare the goats from the yard? No, we had sold them. Months ago. Reverberations of whatever it was shook the house. What in the world, I thought? Half falling from the bunk, I stumbled through the door leading to the back porch, rubbed sleep from my eyes as I walked barefoot and bewildered toward the front yard.

"Dickey!" my mother screamed, coming into sight around the corner of the house. "Hurry! Come quick!"

Suddenly she bolted toward me, weeping, turning to look at the front yard, as if running in a circle, turning completely around again to face me, grabbing at her hair. "I think your daddy's just been killed."

It was just like my mother to imagine the worst, I thought. More than likely Daddy was in town somewhere. But what was the explosion? "Get some water. Quick!" she screamed, lurching toward me. "We've got to put out this fire."

She was uttering nonsense, I thought, and disregarding her command, I walked to the corner of the front yard to see that the Galaxy had been demolished, flames were leaping from the engine and Daddy was inside the car. "God," I said aloud and sprinted to the faucet in the back yard where Mama was already filling up a pail. I grabbed another of the plastic buckets and waited while the meager stream fell, Mama halfway filling one pail before carrying it toward the front yard, water sloshing with her every step. With my bucket only half full, I ran with it to the front yard, reeling at the sight of my father sprawled where the back seat should have been. I poured the water on the flames which hissed in reply but continued to leap from the engine. I ran for more water, stopping this time at a nearer faucet, then returning to the car to extinguish the fire.

Peggy Jean now stood where the door to the car should have been, stooping over Daddy, patting his cheek. "Daddy, listen, Daddy. You're gonna be alright now. We're getting some help. Horace is coming. Everything is gonna be alright."

One hand at my heart, the other to my throat, I assessed the destruction; my father's face splintered by fragments of windshield, pants to his scorched suit shredded at one shin, flesh sliced to bone, torso impaled to car seat by blackened steering wheel, white shirt charred and bloodied beneath the buttons of suit ripped open to reveal intestinal wall. "Oh God'l mighty," I thought, though whether or not I said it, I don't remember, "Oh, God'l mighty, he's going to die." Somehow Horace must hurry. Get him to the hospital. Daddy might be there a long time, but he'd get over this. He couldn't die. God, he couldn't die. Not here. Not now.

"Peggy Jean!" Mama cried. "We've got to call the ambulance." She ran toward the house.

"Mama, I've already called. Horace is coming. He's on his way. And I've called Albert."

My mother stopped in mid-step and returned to the car. "Listen

Daddy," Peggy Jean said. "Listen, I'm right here. Help is coming. You're gonna be alright. You'll be alright."

Suddenly he breathed—or groaned—a long guttural escaping of air. Quickly Peggy Jean was upon him, parting his lips to give mouth-to-mouth resuscitation, but finding his throat blocked by a mass of broken teeth and gums she tried to force air through his nose. "Daddy," she said. "Daddy?" She raised his eyelids, saw nothing but whites, and closed them. She felt for a pulse. "Oh, Mama, he's dead."

"No," Mama wailed. "No, Peggy Jean, no, don't say that. Horace is coming. Albert is coming." She turned to dash toward the house. "Hurry, Horace. Hurry."

"Look, Dickey," Peggy Jean said. "I'd better go see about Mama. She's crazy. She's liable to kill herself. See if you can get him breathing. I can't get any air into his mouth. All his teeth are gone. You're gonna have to breathe into his nose."

"In his nose?"

"Yes, you know how to do mouth-to-nose," she said, glowering at me.

I looked down at my father. His face was the color of dead ashes. Yes, I knew how to do mouth-to-nose, and knew I had to do what I could to revive him. Lowering my face toward him, fighting nausea at the taste of burned flesh, I exhaled into his nose, one hand on his chest to feel the air fill his lungs, raising my head to let the air escape, breathing into him again, his lungs rejecting the air, breathing into him, watching the air escape, breathing in . . .

Minutes later my sister was back. "Peggy Jean, it ain't doing any good," I said.

"Keep doing it," she said and returned to the house.

A neighbor strolled into the yard, a twelve-year-old boy whose face wrinkled with curiosity and revulsion at the sight of the corpse. "Dickey," he asked as if apologizing for interrupting a surgery. "What happened?"

What I wanted to scream was, "What in the hell does it look like happened you stupid son of a bitch?" But instead I gritted my teeth and said grimly, "My father's just been killed."

"Oh," he said, shaking his head, backing away from the yard before turning to walk back across the field. I watched his progress after each rejection of air, time slowing to a crawl until finally the white police car sped up the driveway and skidded to a halt. As if in a dream I walked toward Albert, who leapt from his car and froze in his tracks. "God damn!" he shouted. "God damn!" He pounded his fist into the palm of his hand, tears streaming down his face. "Who would have done this? God damn! Who would have done this?"

He glared at me as if expecting me to answer. I shook my head, my mouth hanging open in disbelief as I realized for the first time that someone had meant for this to happen.

"Oh, God damn," he sobbed again. "Who would've done this?"

I shook my head as if to say that I didn't know.

Chapter Nine

The sun beat down upon the procession walking on the sidewalk beside Mammie's house, freshly polished shoes clopping on the dusty concrete, a train of legs turning to march up the front steps of the Methodist Church. Ahead of us a television camera whirred and clicked among the people standing on either side of the walkway. Through the door of the stone church drifted the moaning of the organ.

No one spoke as we entered the sanctuary crammed with people, some standing at the back of the church, some in the aisles near the walls, others sitting in the choir loft behind the pulpit and the wall of flowers. Those not already standing rose as we entered, staring as we walked hypnotically down the aisle, Albert holding Mama's elbow, Mama dressed in black and crying into her handkerchief, followed by Mammie and my aunts and uncles and Peggy Jean and me, all of us filing in to take seats on the church pews.

Between the altar rail and us sat a copper casket, the same one I'd been asked to approve on the previous afternoon when my Aunt Claudine, Albert's wife, had asked me to walk with her next door to the funeral home. I had followed Horace and her through his office and into a room I'd never before seen, a room filled with caskets, some closed, others opened to reveal their frightful white crepe. Horace had stopped beside the copper one and placed his hand on it. "This is something Fuzzy would have wanted," he said. "Nothing overly expensive. Something in the medium range." He reached for the latch and unfastened it.

"No," I said, stiffening, feeling my legs give way. Horace sensed the reasoning behind my terror. "Fuzzy's not in it," he said softly. "We won't have him in it until you approve."

He opened the casket. Dully, I stared down at the crepe, scarcely believing that only yesterday I had stood in this same funeral home, indifferently pushing around the casket of a stranger, and now suddenly the one downstairs on the embalming table was my father. I nodded my approval, knowing I had to get away from death and my mother's tears and the visitors who had invaded Mammie's house to surround us. But even in my escape of camping out with friends, I could not push away the thoughts of all I'd seen, the car, my father, the GBI men and the sheriff cordoning off the yard, Runt Moore weeping beside a tree, the questions, "Has anybody you know of threatened your father?" The presence of death followed me to the woods. Jim Smith and Buster Shirley and I had lain in the tent, the darkness of the night enclosing us. They had avoided speaking of the murder, obeying adult instructions to distract me, as if mentioning it would set off tears that would be a humiliation for any fourteen-year-old boy, because although sixteen-year-old girls like my sister could cry, a fourteen-year-old boy could not. So we talked of football and girls and avoided the subject of death until finally Jim had grown sleepy enough to reach for the kerosene lantern. "No," I said. "Don't turn it off."

"It's too late," he said. "It's off."

"Y'all aren't going to sleep now, are you?" I protested.

"Yeah, Hoard," Jim said. "I'm sleepy. Go to sleep."

It was pitch black. Every tree limb that fell, every twig that snapped was my ashen father stepping toward me, accusing me of deserting him. Why would he want to hurt me, I told myself. Because maybe this was my fault. Maybe this had something to do with Ronnie Angel. Bootlegging raids. Had I done anything to cause this? I couldn't shake the fear of a visitation.

"Buster?"

"Uumph."

"You're not going to sleep, are you?"

"No."

He stayed awake until I fell asleep a few hours later, but I woke before dawn to spend a final hour or two of misery, too terrified to move, too ashamed of my fear to wake Jim or Buster. And so I replayed the past morning in my mind, as I would again and again, trying to convince myself that it had been a terrible dream. But it was real. The closed casket before me at the church was starkly real and starkly my father's.

"Let us pray," said the minister. I bowed my head, closed my eyes, and clenched my hands across my chest. My mouth was dry, my throat swollen. I fought tears. I must not cry in front of all these people. Too many had already seen me, when I broke down after Albert snatched my father's gun from me. I had picked it from the dresser beside my father's bed even as the GBI agents roamed the yard among the curiosity seekers who craned their necks behind the ropes to see my father's body in the car. I had carried the gun down the hallway, having been struck with the notion that whoever had killed my father would return, hat in hand, wishing to confess, apologizing: "Mrs. Hoard, we never intended to kill him. We just meant to ruin his car," and I would bring the pistol from behind my back and fire every bullet into the man or men who no doubt had stood among the onlookers that very morning. "Dickey," my Aunt Claudine's sister, Dot, shrieked. "What are you doing with that gun?"

Albert heard her and was on me in a flash. "What are you doing, Dickey? Didn't you know that gun was loaded?"

Of course I knew it was loaded. I meant to kill someone with it. He wrested the gun from me. Overwhelmed by a feeling of powerlessness, I wept, "I'm gonna kill the sons of bitches that did this. I'm gonna kill them."

"Hell, Dickey," Albert said. "Whoever did this is back in Detroit or Chicago or wherever it was they come from. They ain't nowhere around here."

I had wept out of rage and frustration then, but couldn't cry now, not in a church full of people. With eyes closed, I tried to think of anything other than the casket before me, copper, suddenly burgundy, George's casket at the same altar five years earlier, brought there from the old funeral home where Daddy had taken us to see George. "His new bed. This is where he's going to sleep."

This! This was nothing like going to sleep. My father's life had been violently blown away. He was dead at forty and no one could stand around the casket and say, "Doesn't he look natural? Doesn't he seem at peace?" The casket had remained closed. "We won't open it," Reverend Ramsey had said to me after I had approved of the casket. "Just remember your father as you last saw him."

"I was at the car," I said, looking up for another suggestion. Reverend Ramsey's face reddened, his brow furrowed, and he turned from me in silence, shaking his head.

"Let not your hearts be troubled," he said now from the pulpit. "Believe in God, believe also in me. . . ."

Why? What good did it do to believe in God? I had tried to pray within an hour of my father's death after my Aunt Claudine had sent me to the backyard with a bag of garbage that I'd put in the burning barrel, lighting some brown paper soaked by the bacon grease from my father's breakfast, watching the flames lengthen and the paper blacken and curl. "God," I had prayed. "If you're real, do something. Do anything." I'd looked up expecting to see an approaching thunderhead, a flash of lightning, a torrent of rain or wind as God showed His anger. But the sky was cloudless, and a mockingbird was singing above me in the trees. God, indeed. Any real God would have prevented all of this, I thought.

The flames from the garbage died down, the smoke from the smoldering papers smelled like burnt flesh. Leaning over, I gagged, convulsively, my empty stomach heaving up nothing.

"And He will give you another counselor, to be with you forever, even the Spirit of truth, whom the world cannot receive, because it neither sees him nor knows him. . . ."

There was no comfort. I glanced up toward the choir loft and saw Jim Smith fidgeting beside one of the football cheerleaders and looking down toward her leg. Abruptly I looked at the back of the pew before me, clenching my teeth; they must not see me cry. Think of something good. Think of—basketball.

Coach Knight, our basketball coach, had stood at the front door of Mammie's house earlier in the afternoon. He had come to speak to me, Mammie had said, and so I entered her living room to greet him and hear him say what an awful thing this all was and how he was surprised to see that I seemed to be handling everything so well. If only I could convince *everyone* I was handling this like a man.

"Two thousand years ago, Jesus steadfastly set his face toward Jerusalem. In less time than a week, he too was struck down. . . ."

Mama wept in the pew before me. From behind me came more sniffling and sobs. But none from me. I gritted my teeth and willed the preacher to quit. "He made his decision, he counted the cost, and yesterday, he paid the full price. And like a sword piercing our hearts, the question which hangs over our heads is this: Did Floyd Hoard die in vain?"

Finally it ended and we rose to file onto the walkway in the pitiless heat. A hand nudged my shoulder. Looking up, I saw the old man dressed in his customary threadbare suit. He said nothing, though he tried, his mouth working like that of a dying fish. He settled for raising two fingers. Tears welled up in my eyes. I raised two fingers as if to say, "Yeah, T.C., me and you."

Chapter Ten

After the funeral, people came by Mammie's house to pay their respects. When a man turns forty, as I have, he can look back and understand that no matter how badly people may want to help, few of them have the foggiest notion of what to say at a time of tragedy. People fail to realize that a fourteen-year-old boy trained to respect his elders might actually take their clichés seriously, that some words offered as blessing turn out to be a curse. "God's got a reason for all this," someone said, as if such atrocities were inspired by the Almighty. Well, if that were the case, then God need not look for me to ever come to His house again. "The Good Lord needed your daddy," said another. To which I thought, "not half as much as I did."

Others instructed me that I had big shoes to fill, that I needed to be strong, that I must work hard to make my daddy proud: "And he will be proud if you grow up to be half the man he was." Even my mother, so consumed with her own grief that she knew less what to say than anyone, said, "You're the man around the house now." The thought horrified and sickened me. For one thing, Mama was the one I expected to forget her own grief and rise to comfort me. It was stupid to think that way, but such are the expectations a fourteen year old can have for his mother. And as for my being a man, I might as well have imagined myself a mongoose. A man was brave, stoic, strong, composed. A man didn't cry. Perhaps the challenges to rise up to premature manhood lay behind my refusal to have a civil conversation with Mama. She tried to talk to me, but every topic, living arrangements, money, transportation to school, a friend who called to wish me well, Mama's applications for a job, reminded me in some way of what we'd lost. It was better not to talk at all, lest rage and grief surface to create unmanly tears. And so whenever talk turned in any way toward Daddy, I cut Mama off. And when she cried or even seemed close to tears, which was often, I left the room. Anything to avoid my own grief. After all, I was expected to be a man.

None of my friends were much help. Most of them disappeared in the hours after the funeral, unwilling, I suppose, to endure the awkwardness of facing me. In fairness to them, if they did come to visit, they most likely missed me, for I was in and out of the house, restless. One person was helpful. Charlotte, older than her years, captain of the cheerleading squad, a senior, saw me pacing the floors and invited me to go for a walk. For an hour or more, she listened with great patience as I recited events of the previous morning. She never changed the subject, never once told me to be brave, never said, "I know how you feel." She merely listened, allowing the escape of enough pent-up anger within me to prevent an explosion. When at dark she left me at the steps of Mammie's house, her shoulders were stooped and her eyes moist from carrying my burden. She offered me her hand and told me she'd be thinking about me. She never again brought up the subject of my father's death, but for one crucial hour she was there.

When Charlotte left, I walked up the stairs to find Peggy Jean with friends in the living room, Mama smoking a cigarette in the kitchen, and Mama's sister, Lanelle, and Mammie working to store leftover food. I left again and walked to Al's. "No," my Aunt Claudine said. "Al isn't back yet. He's off with Carol. Said he'd been through enough today and just needed to get away for a while. You're welcome to stay on over."

I stayed about a half hour, until dark, but grew restless again and returned to Mammie's, walking past the funeral home, now quiet. Ten minutes later I wanted to leave Mammie's again. Peggy Jean had slapped our youngest sister, Vivian, for laughing in the hallway,

Calder insisted on cheering me with a story I didn't feel like hearing, and Mama periodically burst into fresh tears whenever a new face entered the room to offer sympathy.

That night I tossed fitfully in the same bedroom with Lanelle and Calder, who both snored loudly. The windows beside the screened porch were open but no breeze stirred and the heat was stifling. Frequently, the light in the kitchen came on. Mama smoking another a cigarette. Too tired, too hot, too numb, I tossed, determined that the next night, whether Al was home or not, I would stay at his house. And I did. For the next two weeks I stayed there practically every night.

It quickly had become obvious that we would never return to the country house. "Too many memories out there," my Aunt Claudine said. "Everywhere you look out there you see Fuzzy." I had nodded my understanding. How could I ever again walk onto the front porch without seeing him sprawled in the car, body mangled beneath the bloodied suit? And so we left the memories and moved into Mammie's house, Peggy Jean and Claudine to one back bedroom, Mama and Vivian to the other, Mammie keeping her room, which left me, I supposed, the room I'd slept in with Lanelle and Calder, whenever I might choose to stay over. But Mammie would not let me move my belongings in there. One night when I hung up the telephone in the hall outside the kitchen door, I learned why. Mammie was taking in a boarder.

"Now mother, we just don't need anyone else here right now," Mama was saying. "We don't have room and the children need to be here with just family."

"It'll be good for the children to have a man around here," Mammie said. "Especially for Dickey."

Of course she was dooming some poor man from the start, even suggesting that he could enter this house and substitute as my father. But then Mammie didn't know I was listening.

"You don't know what type man he might be. You've got a sixteen-year-old girl living here you've got to think about. And I sure don't want to be left alone with him. Surely he'll understand you didn't have us living here when you took his money. You had no way of knowing this would happen. I'll refund his money to him, myself."

"Imogene, school starts next week and he won't have time to come in here and find himself another place to live, not on such short notice. Now I gave him my word and I'll not go back on it." My mother had never been one to gracefully submit. She protested that he could get a room at the motel until he found something better.

"You know good and well the GBI is filling that place up . . ." Mammie was right. He certainly couldn't stay at the motel. GBI agents had moved into the Crawford Long Inn within hours of the murder, and for more than a week had been at work. They had divulged a few discoveries. Ten to twelve sticks of dynamite had been wired to my father's car. When he turned the ignition switch the bomb exploded. Motives? Vengeance, perhaps; car thieves he had prosecuted, or bootleggers. There was an outside possibility, though they had enough decency to never publicly mention it: domestic problems. Joe Hoard had been living with his brother until a few months before the murder. Had there been harsh words? Hadn't Joe handled dynamite while working for a well drilling company?

Joe had been roused from sleep one night and driven to Atlanta for interrogation. "Now, weren't you jealous of your brother? Weren't you in love with Imogene? You worked for a well drilling company, didn't you? You used dynamite? Come on, Joe, get this off your chest. Why did you kill Fuzzy?" My uncle was so humiliated and despondent that not long afterwards he left Jefferson for good. But everyone was questioned. Even me. "What was the name of the movie you and Joe saw? What was it about? What time did the movie start? Were you there for the beginning of it? Did you come straight home after the movie? On the way back from the movie what did you and Joe talk about? What time did you get home? When Joe drove up in the yard was anything out of place? Had anybody you know threatened your father? Anyone say anything out of the ordinary to you about him?" And though the memory of the conversation with Joe had been triggered—"there comes a time, Dickey," he had said, "when you've got no choice but to kill a man,"—I'd kept silent. It was too ridiculous for me to consider Joe as Daddy's murderer. And how would Joe feel if he thought I had even suspected him? If they were wasting time questioning Joe and me, I figured they had no idea who really killed him. Which was all the more reason to refuse entry to this boarder. Mammie had met him no more than a week or two before the murder. For all we knew he was the man who set the bomb.

But Mammie, contrary to logic, comfort, or safety, kept her word, and on a Sunday afternoon the week before school started, the doorbell rang, rousing me from the living room sofa. At the front screened door stood a man with a large head and wiry body, teeth exposed in a grimace, eyes straining at me from behind thick glasses. He did not reply to my greeting, but looked past me to my mother, who walked down the hall, wiping her hands with a dish cloth, her head cocked with suspicion as she eyed the stranger. Claudine and Vivian followed her. Mouths ajar, they blinked at the man.

"What can we do for you, sir?" Mama asked cautiously.

"I'm—I'm looking for Mrs. Westmoreland."

"Hello, Bobby."

We turned to see Mammie waddling toward us. "I see you made your trip alright. We all want you to come in and make yourself at home and meet the family."

Peggy Jean glowered at him, Claudine and Vivian stared at him, and I accepted his limp handshake, though the one hope I'd entertained about the boarder had been shattered; this was no coach looking for a ball game to break out.

Mammie pushed against the doors of the bedroom, the blinds swinging away from the glass panes. "Now, Bobby, you see it's all ready for you. Dickey will help you bring your things in."

I followed Bobby to his hatchback wagon and reached for a trunk he had set on the sidewalk. "That's—that's not too heavy for you, is it?" Bobby asked.

"Naw," I scoffed. "I used to play football," explanation enough, I figured, for didn't everybody know that football players had to lift weights? And if I could bench press 120 pounds, then a 40-pound trunk was no problem at all.

He scratched his oily head and crinkled his nose at me and busied himself with two large suitcases that he hoisted onto his shoulders and carried up the front stairs, two steps at a time. After only a few trips to the car, we had him settled in what should have been my room.

"Now make yourself at home, Bobby," Mammie said, standing outside the door to his room. "The television is in the living room here and the children will be glad to have you watch it with them any time you can. And you remember where the bathroom is, don't you?"

Bathroom? Why, I'd never even thought about it. This man would share our bathroom. And Mammie had not yet seen how long Peggy Jean could hog a bathroom while primping for school every morning. Competing with five females for one bathroom would be bad enough, but this guy looked like he needed to shave at least twice a day. And he would have to bathe, too. Seven people in one bathroom every morning! No doubt, I was moving my belongings to Al's.

"Now this first night we want you to eat supper with us," said Mammie.

"Oh, no, thank you, Mrs. Westmoreland. I'll—I'll eat something later on downtown."

"Why, we wouldn't hear of it. I've already made you a hamburger. It'll give you time to get to know the children."

"I wouldn't want to impose."

"You won't impose on us, Bobby," I said, looking up to see with great surprise that Mammie was scowling at me. What had I done? Did she really not want him to eat with us? No, she asked him again. And Bobby relented and joined us for supper, boring us with descriptions of the endless hours he had spent sacrificing social life and eyesight in his quest for knowledge. And now after conquering chemistry and physics, he was prepared for his new life, teaching eighth-grade science at Elmwood Elementary.

"Isn't that wonderful!" Mammie said.

I thought not. Eighth-grade science had proved no more interesting than any other science class I'd ever suffered through, and ranked only slightly higher in my interest than algebra.

"I—I just hope I can teach those children something about science."

"Well, I know you will do a wonderful job."

Teach Elmwood children science? Why, the first time Bobby slipped up and called those hoodlums "children" he'd find the tires on his car slashed. They would beat him to death with spitballs within a week. I snickered, almost spewing out a mouthful of tea. At Mama's disapproving glare, I faked a coughing attack, said "excuse me," and reached for another burger. "Pass the ketchup, please, Bobby," I said.

"Now Dickey," Mammie cried in abject horror. "You must call him Mister Sweazy."

"Aw, Mammie," I sneered. "He doesn't want me calling him that. He ain't all that much older than I am. And besides, he's living here." I looked toward Bobby for reinforcement, but none came; he refused to look at me, a smile of self-importance on his face. Why, the son of a bitch, I thought. Come into my house and take my bedroom. Force me to suffer inconvenience. And expect me to treat him like some hotshot professor. It was a good thing I was staying at Al's. Furious, I bolted down the hamburger, gulped down my tea, poured another glass and drained it before rising from the table.

"Where are you going?" asked Mama.

"Can't I even get up from the table around here without someone asking questions? Maybe I'm going to take a crap."

Mister Sweazy's brown face turned white and then purple.

"I just want to know where you're going."

"I'm going to Al's. Where I always go."

"I want you here with us tonight," Mama said.

"I'm going to Al's," I said, scowling defiantly and leaving the room, walking out the front door and letting it slam behind me. I kicked a rock along the sidewalk all the way to my cousin's door. If Mama thought she could make me spend the rest of my life in that house to entertain Bobby Sweazy, she was crazy. In fact, tomorrow, I would move out for good.

For more than an hour Al and I played my baseball game on his living room floor. It was almost dark when the telephone rang. "Dickey, I want you to come on home tonight."

"Mama, I've been staying here practically every night for three weeks. It ain't hurting a thing for me to stay here."

"I want you home."

"Why?"

"Because we need you over here."

"But it's too crowded over there."

"What do you think you're going to do next week when school starts? You can't stay over there?"

"Why not?"

"Because you don't live there. You live here. Now come home right now," she said, and she broke into tears.

"Oh, bull crap!" I shouted into the telephone and slammed it down. "I've got to go home." Al said nothing, but simply shook his head as we picked up the game and I carried it from the air-conditioned room and out into the oppressive heat. Like an inmate on his way to the gallows, I walked to Mammie's, and for the next half hour watched Ed Sullivan until Mammie entered the living room and told us, "No more television tonight. Bobby's had a long drive and he's tired and he's got preplanning at school tomorrow."

"So what am I supposed to do?" I complained. "Go to sleep? My Lord, yes, children, let's all go to sleep. Why, it's nine o'clock."

"Hush your mouth," Mama said. "Get you a book and read it."

"No," I said. "I won't. That's exactly what I won't do; get me a book and read it."

"Find you something to study. You can be reviewing for school."

I sneered and escaped to my only hope for privacy, the bathroom, undressing and getting in the tub, turning on the water and letting it rise. God, I hated it here, I told myself. For a second I thought I might scream or cry. I lay soaking, trying to numb my mind, but

I had been there no more than ten minutes when a knock came at the door.

"What?" I snapped.

"There are other people in this house who might need to get in there," Mama said.

Pulling the rubber plug so hard that I snapped its chain, I hurled the plug at the door and shouted, "Alright."

"And make sure you wash out the tub."

Cursing beneath my breath, I dried and dressed and went to the bottom bunk, face to the wall, sweating beneath a sheet, listening to Mama turn the pages of a booklet by some religious guy. What in the hell she thought the booklet would do was beyond me. Fuming, I listened to the annoying rustling of the pages, the chirping of crickets, the whir of the electric fan, and the snoring of my youngest sister.

Chapter Eleven

The next two nights I lost the battle to stay at Al's. By Wednesday Mama was worn down and didn't bother to phone at all, letting me stay there in peace. But by Thursday evening she had regained her verve and despite my lame protest that it was raining too hard insisted that I come home. When I entered the house, soaked, Bobby said, "Why do you give your mother such a hard time? Did you ever stop to think she might need you here?"

"Yeah," I said, walking away. "I've thought about it." And I had, enough to realize that my life was being sacrificed for this man; he could live here only if another male were present. And his living here meant I had to share a bedroom with my mother and seven-year-old sister, something no fourteen-year-old boy should have to do. But my feelings didn't matter. So, if he couldn't find another place to live, I could. And he'd sure as hell better keep his nose out of my business, I thought, for the less our paths crossed, the better.

Unless, of course, I had to make use of him. And the next evening, facing a predicament, I did. Peggy Jean had accepted a late invitation to attend the football game with friends, leaving me at the last hour with no ride to the stadium. "You can ride with Bobby," Mama said. "He's planning to go."

"Well, won't that be fun," I muttered. But after considering my options—walking, staying home, or riding with Bobby—I opted for a ride.

"That—that would be fine," Bobby said, and so I readied myself in the bathroom, putting on green slacks, a yellow shirt with button-down collar, yellow socks, and my best pair of everyday shoes, brown loafers with tassels. I sprayed on deodorant, brushed my teeth, even gargled with Mammie's mouthwash, knowing that girls would be present, maybe one who took an interest in, flirted with, fell in love with me. As if she were in the mirror, I leaned across the lavatory, lips puckered to kiss her . . .

Someone knocked on the door. "You ready?" Bobby asked.

"Yeah."

"I—I need to get in there before we go."

"Just a minute," I said, brushing my teeth again before walking outside to sit in Bobby's car, parked on the lawn above the brick retaining wall, out of the way of Mama's new car and the blue station wagon, now Peggy Jean's. Bobby opened the door to the driver's side, slid into his seat and cranked the engine. He glanced once over his right shoulder, set the gearstick in reverse, and began backing out of the yard. Even without looking, I could sense he'd forgot about the wall. "Look out!" I cried, too late, feeling the thump and hearing the scrape of metal on brick.

"Goodness!" Bobby gasped, leaping out to inspect the damage. I emerged from the passenger side and circled the car; the left front wheel was on the lawn, the back wheel on the sidewalk, the chassis lodged on the bricks.

"Looks to me like you're stuck," I surmised, failing to catch what Bobby muttered under his breath. He got back in the car and tried to drive it backwards. The front tires spun on the grass and dug into the earth.

"You're digging up the lawn," I protested, but he continued racing his engine and spinning the tires. "Hey, Mister Sweazy, you're digging a hole."

"Push," he screamed, a purple vein bulging on his forehead.

I pushed, but failed to get traction on the rain soaked grass. The earth smelled as if it had been periodically visited by the neighborhood dogs. "It's no use," I hollered. "You're stuck."

Bobby changed to a forward gear, raced the engine and burned rubber on the sidewalk. Finally he gave up and lay his head against the steering column. "Maybe Mama would let you drive her car, if you—"

What I'd intended to say was, "if you promise to be careful," but when he lifted his head and glared at me, I said, "if you—ask her." The vein in his neck was changing colors.

I shrugged innocently and said, "She'd probably let you."

Over the hill atop Martin Street drove Marcus Anderson in his white Mustang. He waved and slowed the car to a halt, parking along the sidewalk. He emerged and walked toward me. "Are y'all having some trouble?"

"We sure are," I said, pointing with my thumb at Bobby, who was shaking his head in the negative. "He got his car stuck on the wall."

"I see," replied Marcus. Pushing his glasses up on his nose, rubbing his lips with a finger and thumb, he surveyed the problem. "Try turning your wheels this way," he suggested, using his hands to motion clockwise, "and go forward."

Bobby sullenly followed the directions, and though it seemed nothing constructive had occurred, Marcus seemed satisfied. "Now just put it in reverse and straighten up your wheels and we'll see if we can't push you off." Marcus and I pushed, me standing in the foul earth to gain a footing. The car dislodged and Bobby backed it into the street.

"Boy, thanks, Marcus," I said, following him to his Mustang. "I'm sure glad you came by."

"Glad to help. I thought I'd ride by. I was looking for someone to ride to the game with me."

"Man, I wished I'd thought to call you," I said. "I figured you had a date."

"Ha! I wish. But we don't always get our wishes, do we? Come on and let's ride."

"Well," I said, glancing over my shoulder at the skulking boarder. "I'd like to, but I'm supposed to be riding with him."

Marcus lowered his voice. "Is he your cousin?"

"No, he's a boarder."

Marcus cocked his head and curled his lip and said, "I don't understand."

"He rents the front room. He's a teacher up at Elmwood."

For a few seconds Marcus stared at me. As perceptive in sizing up the trap I was in as he'd been at sizing up the car's, he nodded almost imperceptibly, grunted, and said, "Damn. Well, some other time, then."

"Next week, Marcus," I said. "Can you drive up to North Habersham next week?"

"I might could. I can ask. We'll plan on it, anyway."

He drove off and I returned to Bobby's car, swinging my leg inside, catching a whiff of a rank odor. I sniffed the air. "You smell anything?" I asked.

"No," Bobby replied, his face still flushed. I checked my shoes for the remnants of a squashed turd, but no, the soles looked clean. With the windows open and the car moving, I no longer smelled it, but when we arrived at the stadium I caught the stench again when getting out of the car. Grabbing my right ankle, I pulled it across my left knee and sniffed. "Egad!" I cried, coughing. I sniffed at the other shoe.

"What's the matter?"

"I stepped in something," I said, and for a moment considered asking him to take me home for more shoes. But then, getting here once had proved hard enough. Another trip and I might not see the game at all. Besides, he was in too ill a mood for granting a favor. He slammed the door and slunk toward the ticket booth. I followed, scuffing my feet on the pavement, hoping to scrape away the origin of the smell. Presenting my student pass I'd bought earlier that day, I waited inside the gate.

"Hi, Dickey," breathed a voice. Turning, I saw two girls smiling at me. I smiled back and noticed that both of them blushed. My lord, they had both sprouted breasts over the summer. They walked— they'd never walked with such oscillations in ninth grade—along the promenade between the swimming pool and the press box, turning to step down into the student section of the grandstand. Somehow, some way, I knew I must escape from Bobby; no way could I sit with a weed when flowers bloomed all around. When he entered the gate, I followed him as far as the press box before mustering my courage and saying, "I'd like to sit with my friends." He frowned, his teeth resting on his lower lip, and for a second I almost felt sorry for him. He'd been in town less than a week and probably didn't know a soul. But those girls!

"Alright," he said. "I'll meet you right here after the game."

I sauntered toward the student section and sat behind the girls, tapping the shoulder of one, a blonde, who turned in her seat and leaned on her elbow, her nose near my feet. "Are you ready for school to start, Dickey?" she asked.

Not wanting my voice to squeak, I took a deep breath and—was it my imagination, or did I smell dog shit? Pressing my heels against the concrete, as far as possible from her nose, I stared at the field, hoping to divert her attention from me. "Naw, naw," I said. "I wish school was out for another month."

"Oh, I don't. I'm so ready for it to start. I've been so bored all summer."

Her companion decided to join the conversation at my ankles. "Me, too," she said. "I have done absolutely nothing the entire vacation except watch television and shell peas. I got so sick of peas."

"We did go to Daytona for a week," said the other. "But it rained, and when it didn't rain it was so crowded."

"We didn't go anywhere. I mean it has been a horrible summer. Dickey, how was your summer?"

"It wasn't all that great a summer," I said.

"No," she said, biting her lip. "I guess not. I'm sorry."

"That's alright," I said, waiting on them to look toward the field before slipping away to climb the steps. I stopped at a water fountain near the pool gates, and after looking around to make sure no one was watching, kicked my shoes beneath a cedar bush. In my stocking feet I returned to sit behind the two girls now joined by several others. "Dickey!" one girl exclaimed, "Where are your shoes?"

Blue-eyed blondes and brown-eyed brunettes looked toward my feet. Lips moist with pink lipstick broke into smiles. "My shoes? I don't know. I must have left them at home," I said, laughing to cover my humiliation. The girls giggled and tapped shoulders to make sure everyone had seen me. But they were soon distracted by the cheerleaders below and started yelling with them, "What kind of Dragons? Fighting Dragons! . . ."

The Fighting Dragons killed White County 38–0. Jack Kesler scored four touchdowns, my sophomore classmate Gus Thompson scored one, Benny Durden blocked a punt, all the sophomores played, and the girls cheered, sometimes asking dumb questions like, "Do we have the ball?" or "Did we get a home run?" but understanding enough to let me know they knew a hero when they saw one. "Number twenty-one. Isn't that Jim Smith? He just made a tackle."

"Boy, Jim's really good, isn't he?"

"Just think of how good he'll be when he's a senior."

I ached to be on the field. My father had been ashamed of me for quitting. He'd sure be ashamed to see me watching with girls. Everyone seemed ashamed of me, judging by their questions: "Dickey, why aren't you down there? Didn't you play last year? Did you quit the team?"

Shortly before the game ended, I returned to the bush and found my shoes and watched the final seconds from the top of the stands, waiting for Bobby to ascend the steps. We pressed through the crowd, reaching the front gate the same time as many of the football players, strutting proudly, flaunting their weariness and their bruises, blue jerseys spoiling the air, people pressing in among them, patting their backs and hugging the sweaty bodies of knights after battle searching out their fair maidens for the rewards offered—embraces, kisses, late trips to Athens for a hamburger, perhaps even some parking at the Big Oaks. And I, a weakling unfit for the sport of men, walked toward the car with Bobby Sweazy, wishing more than ever that I had never quit the football team.

My regrets intensified Monday at cross-country practice. After

Coach Keen issued us shoes and sweats, he set us to running a course more than two miles long. "I don't care how you finish this first day," he had told us, "even if it means walking or crawling in. But whatever you do, don't quit."

The sun beat down from between high cotton clouds, the air humid. Blinking away sweat I looked for the lead runners, who had gained a three- or four-hundred-yard advantage, having turned the corner of the baseball field's gray walls to head up the road beside the football stadium. I plodded along, finally turning the corner to approach the long hill, forcing myself to keep moving. No longer did my feet seem to propel me forward; instead the paved road rolled beneath me like a great conveyor belt carrying fragments of beer bottles and flattened cigarette butts. I reached the top of the hill and the level paved lot outside the swimming pool fence, stumbling and nearly falling when climbing the steep bank to reach a winding dirt road behind the pool. "Look for the tractor tire and turn left," Coach Keen had told us when describing the course, and for a second I panicked: Where the hell was the tractor tire? Where were the other runners? Had I made a wrong turn somewhere to get off course? Suddenly my stomach heaved cold fluid into my mouth. Stopping, hands on knees, I puked on the road, aware of a few stragglers who passed, making a wide arc around me and the blotted earth. When the heaving ceased and my vision cleared, I trailed the stragglers around another bend in the dirt road and turned beside the huge tire to face yet another hill. At its crest stood Coach Keen, clipboard in one hand, stopwatch in the other, black cord to the stopwatch hanging around his neck, muscles bulging tightly against the short sleeves of his white shirt. Surely, I thought, as I ascended toward him, this man will take one look at me, see that I'm near death, and tell me, "You've had enough, Dickey. Stop right now and walk over to the shade." But he hardly noticed me when I passed, his stern gaze fixed on the stopwatch. "Twelve-thirty-seven," he said, as I passed by and suddenly found myself racing downhill, gaining speed, almost out of control, slowing my pace to keep from losing my balance, arriving again at the road beside the stadium. My lungs burned, calves cramped. I thrashed my arms about hoping to stop the aching in my shoulders.

A car horn blared. Looking up, I saw Truckie Myers drive past, his car loaded with football players on their way to practice. Benny Durden waved at me and hollered out, "Let's pick up the pace, Hoard."

"Bastards," I muttered. Bastards with noses in the air because they'd won the football game. Everybody in town was talking about it. Big winners. Thirty-eight-to-zero winners. And me? I was a loser, struggling to avoid finishing dead last, a loser who had puked up whatever guts he had on a dirt road, a loser who wanted only to quit this race. Quit, an inner voice told me, arguing with other voices that urged me on. *Whatever you do, don't quit. Even if you have to walk in this first day, don't quit, or you'll wind up quitting everything, son, like you quit football*, the voices in my ear driving me forward until with a gasp I crossed the finish line third from last.

Chapter
Twelve

It's one thing for a boy to decide for himself that he wants to run cross country to gain stamina for basketball season. He can then view each practice as an opportunity to improve, a chance to reach his dream. It's another thing for adults in authority to say that either the boy run cross country or forfeit his right to play basketball, which then makes cross country an unjust punishment inflicted by those seeking to build a football dynasty. A pain chosen hurts less than a pain inflicted. And cross country was an infliction, a daily ordeal that hung like a pall over my life. "I start dreading it everyday about lunch," I told Marcus a month into the school year. Said he: "You're lucky. I wake up dreading it."

Perhaps if some acclaim had accompanied the sport, we could have endured it better. But as Tony Duke said, "Some people at school don't even know we have a cross-country team. Much less an undefeated one." But they sure knew we had an undefeated football team. Everybody in town was talking. Merchants displayed posters in their store windows and feted the team to steak dinners. Fans gathered on Monday nights to watch the game film at the Booster's Club. Three thousand people and more attended games. Jefferson was drunk on football.

In contrast, a half-dozen spectators, none of them from Jefferson, would watch our cross-country team perform each Friday at the Atlanta Waterworks. "Even my mama wouldn't ride all the way to

Atlanta to see me run," Tony said. "And who can blame her. Fifteen minutes and its over." Actually for Tony it took less than twelve minutes to complete the course, two laps around a lake, two ascents of Dodd Dam, the steep incline appropriately named, said Marcus, "because that's exactly what I say every time I run up it," two descents of Lyle's Leap, finally gasping across Fowlkes Finish. And then came my favorite time of the week, the Friday evening ride back to Jefferson. We would scatter long enough for supper, then regather for the football game. Because the school neither owned nor had access to a van, the cross-country team made its Friday trips in three cars, Coach Keen's station wagon and the vehicles of two seniors. I was quick each Friday to secure my ride with Tony or Marcus, and on the way home, we relaxed by joking, singing along with the radio, or disparaging one another.

"You're crazy, Tony. What do you mean you don't mind running out here?"

"Think about it. At practice we run courses longer than this one—and then run alternating paces or a bunch of thirteen-twenties. Or run the hills. Out here we just run the course. And that's it. It's almost like a day off."

"You're crazy, man. Next thing you'll be saying is you actually like cross country—Lord, like Petey Paul."

"Don't be talking about Coach Keen's pet."

"Coach Keen just loves Petey Paul," I said.

"If you could run like Petey Paul he'd love you, too."

"He can love who he wants to," said Marcus. "I'm not telling him any different."

"What are you so scared of Coach Keen for?" asked Butch Graham. "He puts on his britches every morning the same as you."

"I doubt it," Marcus said. "He probably says, 'Pants, get on,' and they come crawling up his legs . . ."

Looking back, I realize that some of my best friendships were forged during our Friday travels while lamenting our common misery. And yet despite the camaraderie, I felt dissatisfied. Something was missing from my life. No doubt, I thought, if I found a girlfriend, I would finally be happy. And the night I discovered the charms of Tessa Halley, I was certain I had unlocked the door to happiness.

The Friday routine was broken the first week of October, when the cross-country meet was moved to Thursday, and I found myself with a Friday night date. It had been planned the previous day before the bell ended third-period English class.

"So what else am I going to do?" Tessa, a cheerleader, was saying to the girl behind her. "I'm gonna have to ride to the game with Jane and we're gonna have to leave late and all, 'cause Jack don't get off work till like six, you know, and I'm not supposed to be riding with them, you know. Like everybody thinks I'm riding with my parents."

She sighed, lifting both palms, rolling her eyes. Her feet were in the aisle beside my desk, her skirt above her knees. She had a scar on one knee, and a slight run in her hose at one thigh. When I looked up from her legs and saw that she was staring at me, I blushed, and looked away. At the time it never occurred to me that she intended for me to both hear her conversation and admire her legs.

She raised her fingers to brush her red hair away from her ears and smiled at me. "Are you going to the game?" she asked.

As I'd done the past four weeks, I would ride with my teammates. But impulsively I lied. "No," I said, thinking myself bold. "I'd sure like to go, but I don't have a ride."

"Well, you can ride with us."

I caught my breath, studying her eyes for signs of sarcasm. She stroked her cheek and smiled. "I'd—uh—I'd like to ride," I heard myself tell her.

With a glint in her eye she leaned toward me and purred, "Okay. You can ride, but don't tell anybody. Charlotte can't find out." The girl behind her, who'd been listening to every word, smiled innocuously.

"Charlotte?" I asked.

"Yeah, you know, Charlotte, like the cheerleading captain, Charlotte. If she finds out I didn't ride with my parents I'll get my little ass kicked off the cheerleading squad. And if I get my little ass kicked off the cheerleading squad, and my mother finds out, and I mean, you know, she'll like wonder why her daughter isn't down on the field with the rest of the cheerleaders, and might just want to know why, don't you think, and then she'll kill me—or worse than that ground me."

"I won't tell anybody," I said, glancing back at the girl behind her.

"We'll have to figure out a place to meet where nobody'll see us."

"What about the drug store?"

"Are you crazy?" she hooted, drawing the annoyed gazes of our classmates and a wrathful stare from Mrs. Smith, our teacher. I hid my forehead behind my hands, keeping silent until the class volume had risen.

"Are you some kind of yoyo?" she hissed. "Somebody will see me down at the drug store. I mean, you know, like everybody knows me there. Just meet us on the square. We'll drive by and pick you up."

I balked at the image of hanging out at the square. People seeing me might stop and ask too many questions. "I tell you what. Just meet me at Marlowe's Cafe."

She glowered. "No, really," I said. "Y'all can just drive by, and I'll be sitting at the window and come right out when y'all get there. You won't even have to get out of the car."

"Okay," she said. "We'll meet there right after six. But be there before six in case Jack can get off work early. And remember. Nobody'd better find out."

"I won't say a word."

And I didn't, though sorely tempted on the way to the cross-country meet that afternoon to tell Marcus and Tony. But I kept my word, harboring the wonderful secret, hardly able to sleep that night, scenarios playing themselves out in my mind. A real date, my first, unless I counted last year's Twerp Dance when Joe had driven with my date sitting between us. Tomorrow night, I might find myself in the back seat with Tessa Halley. But then suppose Tessa had invited me merely out of friendship? Suppose they rode up, this Jack fellow driving, Jane beside him, and Tessa riding shotgun in the front? What would I do? Sit alone in the back seat and act as though I'd never expected anything different? Or invite her to sit in back? But most likely, she would already be there. What then? Rumor had it that Tessa would make out. But would she with me? And how would I know? How would I initiate it? Simply lean over and smack her on the lips? Or ask permission: "Tessa, you look so very beautiful tonight, my darling, that I simply must kiss you. May I?" She'd probably slap my head off, or worse, laugh at me.

The possibilities had played themselves out in my dreams the previous night and still haunted me as I sipped at the soft drink at Marlowe's; the drink was too sweet, cloying my mouth with a strong aftertaste. I exhaled into my cupped hand and tried to sniff my breath, removing from my shirt pocket a stick of gum, unwrapping it, wadding it into my mouth, stealing another glance at the clock—nearly a quarter till seven. Tessa had told me to be here before six. Maybe she had no intentions of showing up at all. Why she might be in the cheerleaders' van right now, halfway to Morgan County, eliciting laughter with her account of standing me up: "That idiot Dickey Hoard is at Marlowe's Cafe right now. That idiot really believed me yesterday when I told him I was riding to the game with you, Jane?"

"No! Really?"

"Yeah. Can you believe he thought I'd risk getting kicked off cheerleading by skipping out with him and your boyfriend?"

"He's such a—twerp. Serves him right, the way he's always acting. Nobody likes him." Peggy Jean had often said it. Maybe she was right.

I shifted nervously at the front booth, sipping at the soft drink while looking out the front window. Evening shadows stretched across Lee Street. Traffic was thin. Several people sat toward the back of the cafe —a woman with gray hair and a man with none, who were eating supper at a booth and talking with a few men who drank coffee at the same table where my father had always sat. Did they suspect my disgrace? I strained to hear their voices:

"Don't look like they ever will."

"People can get away with anything these days."

"If they did catch anybody they ought to give him the chair."

"You know they're talking about doing away with the electric chair. Do away with all capital punishment. Call it cruel and unusual punishment."

"You don't reckon getting blown up in your car isn't cruel and unusual?"

Sighing, I stared out the window and wondered what Daddy would have said if he'd ever caught me plotting such a scheme. Lying to my mother had always been serious enough for punishment by the belt. She had caught me off guard at the supper table by asking me of my plans for the night. "I'm going to the game."

"Who are you riding with?"

"Some guy named Jack," I said, taking a bite of green beans, immediately regretting that I'd told the truth.

"I don't believe I know anybody named Jack."

"No," I said. "I don't think you know him."

"Well, who is he?"

"He's one of the cheerleader's boyfriends."

"What grade is he in?"

"I think he's graduated already."

"Well I don't think I want you going off with somebody that old. I don't mind you riding with Marcus or Tony. But I don't know this boy. He's sounds like he's too old."

A wave of panic swept over me; my one chance for a date and Mama had suddenly taken an interest in my nocturnal activities. I had to meet Tessa. Even if it meant lying. "Well, Marcus is going," I said, not exactly a lie; Marcus was certainly going to the game, but not with Jack. "And Tony. He's going."

"Is this boy coming by here to pick you up?"

"No, there's so many of us riding, he's picking us up downtown. He doesn't have time to go by everybody's house."

Mammie interrupted to tell me, "You should never get in the car with boys who drink beer. But if you should get in the car and find out they are drinking beer, you must say, 'Now you're just going to have to let me out right now. I don't ride with anybody that's drinking beer.'"

"Good lord, Mammie," I said. "I ain't riding with nobody like that." I stood up as calmly as possible and went into the bathroom and brushed my teeth, plotting my course of action. My best move would be to leave as quickly as possible and avoid more questions. I strolled back into the kitchen, finished the iced tea in my glass, and told Mama I was leaving.

"I think I'd better take you downtown," Mama said. I glanced at her plate; she'd only half finished her meal, and she'd sure want to eat all her chicken before she took me.

"Can't wait," I said. "I've got to go right now. He's picking us up at 5:30."

"I haven't said yet that you could go."

"Well, I am going," I said, walking out the back door, hearing Mammie begin a repeat of her lecture.

"Dickey, come back here," Mama demanded, but too late, I was gone, out the back door, running to the lane between Colonel Davis's garage and his car shed, hiding between the buildings and looking toward Mammie's door. No one emerged. I breathed a sigh of relief and walked the back street to Brown's Store and from there past the square and to Marlowe's. I ordered a soft drink and tried to appear inconspicuous. But an hour had passed with me sitting by the window and still no Tessa. Five after seven. Must I hide out at the motel until eleven o'clock or so? I sure couldn't go home. Not after all those lies. Mama would find out the whole story.

Almost ten after seven. Along the curbing outside, a car stopped. In the front seat sat Jane and her boyfriend, in the back seat Tessa. My heart leaped, partly in relief, partly in fear. I ambled out to the car, trying to appear composed as I opened the back door and said, "Hi."

"You dumbass!" Tessa shrieked, reaching up and grabbing me by the collar and pulling me into the back seat. "Do you want everybody to see us?"

Embarrassed at her outburst, I stammered, "No, no."

"Damn it, Jack, would you hurry up!" she spat. "Would you please get the hell out of town before the whole world sees us."

Jack smiled mockingly. "Now, now, Tessa, you wouldn't want me to speed now, would you?"

"You're damned right I want you to speed, you asshole. You speed everywhere else you go. You can speed to this goddamned ballgame," she raved before turning to smile sweetly at me and say, "Pardon my French."

"It's alright."

"Don't worry, Tessa. I'll get you to the football game before this Charlotte Almighty kicks you off the cheerleading squad."

I sat uncomfortably, quietly trying to clear my throat while Tessa alternated between raving at Jack and explaining to me, "We wouldn't have been so late, but Jack here had to stop at the package store and buy him some beer." Suddenly I realized that she was in the middle of the seat with her leg touching mine. I swallowed hard. "And to top everything off, I got to rushing around so bad I didn't have time to change. I'm gonna have to dress in the back seat."

"Well, let me adjust my rearview mirror," said Jack, his girlfriend responding with an elbow to his arm.

Suppressing a gasp I said, "I—I'll turn my head."

"Damn!" she hollered. "What do you think I'm gonna do? Strip down right here in front of all of you?"

"We had hoped so," said Jack, bracing himself for another punch from Jane.

"I've got my cheerleading panties on. All I've got to do is slip my skirt on over them."

I twittered, relieved that Tessa, who had once publicly taunted me that I wouldn't know what to do if some girl stripped naked and "offered it to me" wouldn't be the one to find out how right she was. She unzipped the jeans and slid them off. I observed her movements from the corner of my eye, my heart beating rapidly, as she pulled the uniform over her blouse and tossed the two straps behind her shoulders. "Can you get these?" she said.

"Sure," I said, trying to prevent my voice from quaking and fingers from trembling as she turned her back to me. I fastened the buttons of the straps and sat back in the seat, propping my arm behind her head. She leaned back, nestling herself against my shoulder. In the twilight she was beautiful, her short red hair almost brown in the fading light, her lips shaded and moistened by pink lipstick. She had never looked so beautiful in English class. Sensing my gaze, she turned her face toward mine and smiled. Was she teasing me? Did she want me to kiss her? Slowly I lowered my mouth toward hers, my eyes open to make sure I found the target. Her eyes closed, her lips parted, her smile became a receptive kiss, her mouth soft, playful, wonderful. Never in my wildest daydreams had I imagined such a sensation. Now I knew. Now I knew why boys spent their money on girls at the drug store, why they gave them rings, why they would fight over a girl. I would risk Mama's wrath any day for such kisses from Tessa Halley. Raising my head from hers, I looked at her again. She smiled dreamily and lay her head against my shoulder. I was in love.

With whom was I in love I now realize is questionable. If Tessa had been Maria Jensen or either of the two blondes I'd sat behind at the first football game, or even a ten-dollar whore, it wouldn't have mattered. What mattered was that someone attractive, and in Tessa's case, accepted well enough by others to be elected cheerleader, had elevated my status by letting me know I was worth kissing. The rush of emotions that I mistook as love came not so much from my kissing her as from her kissing me.

If only my teammates could see me now, I thought, as her lips played on mine. Problem was, they couldn't, unless someone told. And I had been sworn to secrecy.

The next afternoon I lay on the couch, paying scarce attention to the World Series game on television, preferring to savor the memories of the previous night, of Tessa's hand on my face, of her embraces, of her soft kisses the entire ride home. So absorbed was I in the reveries that when Claudine and Vivian entered the living room to stand beside the television and threaten to change the channel, I merely grunted, hugging the pillow. "Dickey," said Claudine, poised to run. "We're changing the channel." She changed to the station playing "Astro-Boy." "We changed the channel."

I turned to face the back of the couch.

"We changed the channel. We changed the channel," chanted Vivian.

"Dickey, are you sick?"

Yes. Lovesick. So moonstruck that I was actually looking forward to Monday when I could see Tessa again. So what if Monday also brought cross-country practice. I could endure a week of pain if I knew that next Friday night would bring a repeat of such bliss.

That evening, I gathered up a change of clothes and left to spend the night with Andrew, something I could do now that Bobby had taken to going home on weekends. Andrew was also a sophomore and a member of the football team, a distinction that had landed him the prize of a steady girlfriend, a senior already announced for the homecoming court.

After entertaining ourselves late that night by sitting in our underwear in the middle of the road beside his house, waiting for the headlights of cars to crest the hill before running to dive in the shrubbery, we cooked some hot dogs for a snack, and then went to bed. Lying there, I asked Andrew, "What do you think about going steady?"

"You asking me to go steady? You some kind of queer or something?" he laughed. His laugh always sounded like a maniacal trip up and down a musical scale.

"You know what I mean. Do you like going steady with Patricia?"

"Hell, yeah, I like it."

"What do you like about it?"

He was silent for a few seconds, which meant that he would answer seriously. "Well," he said. "It's sort of like this: It's nice not having to worry all the time about getting a date. You don't have to make all these elaborate plans. Sometimes I'll just call her up at the last minute and ask if she wants to go out, and sometimes she doesn't want to do much of anything, so we just sit around her house and watch T.V. and when her mom and dad leave the room we make out." He grabbed my arm and punched it, laughing.

"You think it's good to go steady then, huh?"

"Yeah, I like it. You'd like it, too, Hoard. You could go steady if you weren't such a picky bastard."

For a while I lay silently, musing about the previous night, a smile crossing my face; Monday I would ask Tessa to go steady. But what could I give her? I had no ring, no athletic jacket, and no job to earn money to buy her Cokes at the drug store. "Say, Andrew," I asked. "When you asked Patricia to go steady, what did you give her? I mean, you don't have a football jacket or a class ring."

"I went and shelled out some pretty big bucks at a jewelers for a ring. Why are you asking?"

"Just wondering."

"Just wondering, my ass. I don't buy that. You're asking all this for a reason. Now what is it?"

"Oh, it's nothing really."

Andrew sat up in bed and grabbed my t-shirt and said, "You're hiding something, Hoard. Are you going steady?"

"No."

"Are you asking somebody to go steady?"

"Well—"

"Damn you, Hoard. You are. Who?"

"No, it's nothing like that," I said, my resistance weakening, the wonderful secret wanting to escape. "Look, I can tell you this much. I had a date last night."

"Who with?"

"That's what I can't tell you. If anybody finds out she'll get in trouble."

"What's the matter? Is she a fourth grader or something?" he asked, laughing again. "Listen, Hoard, I'm not going to tell anybody."

"I promised not to say anything."

"Some friend. I tell you about all my dates, don't I? Don't I?"

"Yeah, I guess—"

"You have one lousy date and you think I'm gonna spread it all over the school. I swear on a stack of Bibles it'll never leave this room. Now who was it?"

"You swear you won't tell anybody?"

"I swear it. I swear. Now tell me."

I balked before answering. "Tessa."

"Tessa!" he hollered, grabbing my shirt and laughing, stifling his laughter and listening to make sure his outburst hadn't waked his parents. "You!" he whispered. "Damn you, Hoard! You went out with Tessa Halley?"

"Yeah," I said, glowing at his approval.

"Did you ride home from the ballgame with her?"

"Yeah."

"Did y'all do anything?"

"We just made out, is all," I said, feeling a burst of energy at the secret's release, knowing that having now proved myself to be one of the fellows, loved by a cheerleader, I could hold my head up high at Jefferson High School. Monday, I would ask Tessa to go steady. But I couldn't wait until Monday to talk to her. The next afternoon I phoned her, and asked her to ride home with me from the next football game.

"You don't have a car."

"I'll find us a ride," I said. "First thing in the morning."

"We'll see," she said.

Monday morning I cornered Tony in the hallway before school and pleaded with him to find a date for Friday. He promised to try. Taking his promise as confirmation, I swaggered down the hall when third period approached, turning the corner to see Big Ed sloughing toward me, his shirttail out in back, his face lighting up when he saw me.

"Hey, Hoard," he bellowed, loud enough for practically everyone in the hall to hear. "I heard about you and Halley Friday night."

The blood in my face seemed to drain into my neck. My mouth hung open. How did Big Ed know? Andrew! Damn Andrew! He'd run his mouth. And if Big Ed, seldom told any choice gossip, had heard, why the whole school must know. Suddenly shaken, I walked into class, catching a few knowing smiles from the girls behind me. My only hope was that Tessa hadn't learned that the secret was out. But seconds after the tardy bell, Tessa entered, her face crimson and contorted. Scowling, she threw down her books and slid her desk violently backward into the desk behind her.

"There will be no more outbursts like that, young lady," Mrs. Smith said, her reprimand hardly noticed by the culprit, who snarled at me through clenched teeth, "If Charlotte finds out . . ."

The girls behind me giggled and I decided it best to forget the subject of a ride to Friday night's game. Humiliated by her demonstration, I stared down at the desktop and the carved initials of scholars past. So much for courtship and falling in love. The purring kitten of Friday had suddenly become a snarling cat. And, in the broad light of Monday morning, she didn't look very appealing at all.

Chapter
Thirteen

Every day I pushed myself to improve my racing times, venting my rage on the cross-country course, as if improving my speed might somehow punish the world that had cost me my father. "I'll show them," I thought, never quite able to figure out exactly what I thought I might show them, perhaps that I could rise above commonality, or maybe only rise to commonality, for a part of me wanted only to be ordinary and accepted by my peers, though I sensed that to be accepted, one had to excel in some area. For me, that area was sports. And so I worked to improve. Coach Keen had told us that a distance runner should "think of anything but running: a trip to the mountains, homework assignments, a song you like on the radio. . . ." I set my mind on music or girls, most frequently Tessa Halley, whose only further acknowledgment of my existence had come within a week of our date when she flashed a senior ring at me so I'd know she was going steady. Maybe she thought I'd be jealous. But all I felt was pity for the poor idiot who'd wasted his money on a ring, bitterness toward Tessa for embarrassing me, and disgust for myself— what in the world had I ever seen in her? My bitterness propelled me toward basketball season, when I would prove to Tessa and all girls everywhere that I was worth loving.

Finally, in early November, cross-country season ended. I sat against the wall at the bottom of the grandstands listening to Coach Keen tell those of us who would not run in the state meet, "Don't think that because you're not in the top seven that you haven't contributed to this team. You have pushed the man ahead of you who has then pushed the man ahead of him and so on up the line until you've made even Petey better than he could have been otherwise. For instance, listen to this. Dickey Hoard—a twelve-thirty-seven two-mile! Who would have thought when we first started that he could ever run it in that? Twelve-thirty-seven! That's amazing!"

I glowed, partly from his affirmation, but mostly from the realization that I had survived the season—that tomorrow afternoon I would be issued a pair of Converse All-Stars and a uniform of the varsity basketball team. Finally, here was something enjoyable to invest my life in, a place to prove my worth—the basketball court. Three weeks later, our season began, and I managed to earn playing time as the first guard off the bench. In my first game I scored six points and created a stir when, in chasing after an errant pass, I disappeared through an open door and down a stairwell, emerging unharmed to courteous applause from both sides of the gym.

The savor of our 53–45 victory and the mild acclaim of scoring six points was quickly spoiled on the Monday after Thanksgiving, the eve of our first home game, when Coach Knight sent a note asking me to meet him in the physical education classroom before practice. Nervous, I'd entered the room to find him already dressed in his ragged white sweatshirt, a whistle dangling from his neck. He looked up at me from behind the desk, his eyes stern as he said, "Dickey, I'd like to know where you were Wednesday."

I cleared my throat, searching for the words to explain what had happened when I'd arrived home Wednesday to find Mammie and my sisters in the car, Mama at its door, cigarette clenched between her lips. "I was just about ready to come looking for you, son," she had said. "We're all packed and ready to go."

"Ready to go where?"

"Where we go every Thanksgiving. I'm going to Lanelle's."

"I can't go. I've got basketball practice."

"That's too bad, because you are going with me."

"Mama, I have to be there."

"Where do you think you're going to stay for two nights?"

"I can stay at Al's."

"You're going with us. All year long I set my schedule around y'all. I can't do anything, I can't go anywhere because of y'alls activities. And then one time in the year when I do decide I want to do something," she said, breaking into tears, looking up and sobbing, "Oh, Fuzzy."

"Hell fire. Hell fire," I hollered. "Get in the damned car right now, and let's go."

"Do you want me to call Coach Knight and tell—"

"Hell no," I said, an image flashing into my mind of Mama weeping and griping at Coach Knight for calling a practice on Thanksgiving Eve. The further she stayed from him, the better. "I don't want you going anywhere near Coach Knight. Let's just go."

And so we had left town and words of explanation didn't seem to come as I stood before Coach Knight. "I asked Tony and Marcus where you were," he said, "and they told me they thought you were coming to practice."

"Yes, sir, I was, but when I got home I found out I had to go to my aunt's."

"Well, I don't think I'm asking too much of you boys to have you call and let me know things like that."

"No, sir," I said, staring at the floor.

"I'm going to have to discipline you. You'll have to run extra zigzags after practice today. And another thing: you know I can't very well put you in the game tomorrow night ahead of Gus and Andrew and these other boys who stayed around to practice, can I?"

"No, sir," I said, my heart sinking at the prospects of watching our home opener from the bench.

At the end of practice I suffered through the zigzags. Starting at one baseline, we ran to the free-throw line and back, to mid-court and back, to the far free-throw line and back, to the far baseline and back, each "zigzag" timed to assure that we ran it within thirty seconds. I ran three of them with the team and five more as punishment, then collapsed on the floor after the final one, gasping for breath, exhausted by the effort, and made a vow that never again would I obey an order from my mother.

But the worst punishment came Tuesday night when I sat on the bench while every member of the squad entered the game before me, until finally, with two minutes left in the first half, Coach Knight called my name. By the time the buzzer sounded my entry, there was less than a minute left. Even then, I managed to score a basket, giving me hope that my exile to the bench had ended. But to my dismay I watched the third period and most of the fourth from my chair. Inside two minutes Coach Knight called me again, "Dickey, go in for Andrew and run our red offense. Tell them, nothing but lay-ups."

I relayed the message, understanding that Coach Knight wanted us to protect our two-point lead by forcing South Habersham to commit a foul. And when, with thirty seconds to play, the pass came to me, the last player off the bench, a guard fouled me. One shot, plus a bonus. "Number twenty-two, you're shooting. And a time out, red," the referee said, pointing toward the South Habersham bench, where their coach stood with his hands forming a "T," apparently giving a scrub like me sixty seconds to feel the pressure of the situation.

"Now, boys," Coach Knight said as we huddled around him. "We've got a two-point lead, so whatever happens, if Dickey hits this first free throw, force them to take an outside shot. And even if he misses it and they get the rebound, make them take the outside shot. But, remember, no fouls."

The buzzer sounded us back to the floor, and I walked to the free-throw line. "You'll choke, boy," said one of our opponents as he walked past. The referee handed me the ball, the fans of the visiting team stomped on the wooden bleachers and shrieked, "Miss it, miss it." I dribbled once, twice, and shot—basket. Cheers erupted from the home bleachers. The bonus shot. Another basket. Four-point lead. The noise was piercing.

A South Habersham player brought the ball down court and took a long shot. Basket. Only a two-point lead with less than twenty seconds. Foul in the back court. One of our seniors, our star player,

Butch Graham, went to the line. And though he missed the free throw, it didn't matter. South Habersham failed on their final shot. The game ended, cheerleaders raced onto the court, beautiful Marie Nunnally throwing her arms around me. I lifted her off the floor and held her close, elated at the adulation in her eyes.

My teammates swarmed me. "Way to go, Hoard," Tony said. "You pulled us out."

"Ice man," said Marcus. "You amaze me, boy. You've got ice water in your veins."

The entire team pressed against me to congratulate me. Except for one, Butch Graham, who walked off the court with his girlfriend. At the time I figured he was having girl problems; his head was down, and he was scowling as if we'd lost the game. At the time it didn't occur to me that he might have felt embarrassment at having missed his free-throw after watching the young sophomore become a hero. I hardly thought of Butch at all as I basked in my glory. Here was the approval I'd been hoping for. Only in looking back could I suspect that what happened in the final minutes of our next game had anything to do with jealously. But when Coach Knight removed Butch from the lineup, instead of going to the bench, Butch threw a towel onto the court and stomped up several rows of bleachers to sit with his girlfriend until the game ended, inciting Coach Knight to confront him in the locker room as we dressed. When Graham muttered something (neither Marcus nor I could hear what he said), Coach Knight told him, "As of right now, you are no longer on this team," and stormed from the room.

The room fell silent. We watched Butch throw his jersey into his duffel bag. He grabbed up his towel and muttered a profanity. "What are y'all staring at?" he said, and walked out.

"There goes our damned season," Marcus cried. "Work all your life for the big senior year and—"

"Aw, let him go," said Doug Hanson. "How many of y'all got taken out some time during the game? What if we all sat with our girlfriends?"

The next afternoon Marcus and I cruised along the outskirts of

Jefferson, still bemoaning Butch's outburst. "It doesn't make sense," I said. "Suffer all through cross country just so you can play basketball and then get kicked off the team the third game of your senior year. Why did he do it?"

"Just showing his butt, I guess. I guess he just couldn't stand the thought that he could be substituted for."

"Well, do you think Coach Knight will let him come back?"

"I sure hope so. I don't see how we can win without him."

"What'll happen tonight? I mean, who do you think will start?"

"Ha! That's easy. You will."

"Me?" I hooted, and laughed nervously. "I'm just a sophomore."

"So what? You're the only other guard we've got who can get the damned ball up the court."

It was a sobering thought, starting after only three varsity games. "Naw," I said, laughing uneasily at Marcus's prediction, but the gloominess of the team's ill fortune gave way to anxiety as the hour approached for us to leave for Oglethorpe County. When getting on the bus, I paused beside Coach Knight, hoping he might divulge my status, but he said nothing, leaving me to suspect I'd be on the bench when the game started. Not until the team had finished warmup drills and huddled prior to the tipoff did he tell us, "Red, you're at pivot; Tony, you and Doug at forwards; Marcus, you and Dickey at guards."

And so before I had time to worry about it, I found myself on the floor to start the game, struggling against a full court press. Oglethorpe County's team stole passes, stripped the ball from Marcus and me with double-teams, frequently sending me to the free-throw line for foul shots. We ended up losing the game 71–52, and Graham watched smugly from the bleachers, appearing to enjoy the rout.

When the game ended, we trudged downstairs to sit on wooden benches in the locker room and listen as Coach Knight tried to lift our spirits by telling us, "We simply weren't ready for this. It's going to be hard for any team to come in here and win in this old barn. Their court is smaller than regulation size and they used it to their advantage. It's my fault we weren't prepared for their press, but we'll work on it, and we'll get better. As for now, let's just get dressed and go home and put this one behind us."

I sprayed on deodorant and pulled on my trousers, listening to the muffled complaints of my teammates: "Too nasty in there to shower . . . what a lousy dressing room . . . more like a dungeon . . . ," pondering whether Graham's presence in the lineup could have made a difference, wondering if people were blaming me for the lopsided defeat. "Hoard," shouted one of the managers as he bolted down the stairs. "Hoard, you sucker, where are you?" He ignored the annoyed glances of the team members and shouted, "Guess how many points you scored tonight?"

I shrugged and said nothing, concentrating on buttoning my white shirt. "Twenty-five!" he hollered. "Twenty-five points, you sucker. That's a school record." Blushing, I told him it wasn't a school record. I remembered several players who'd scored more.

"Well, it's a team record," he argued. As my teammates responded —"Hoard got twenty-five? Way to go . . . give him a starting job and he's already breaking records . . . ," I suppressed a grin, aware that any vainglory in defeat would insult the team.

After dressing I walked alone to the bus, acknowledging the compliments from members of the girls' team and scanning the bus for a seat. All seats near the back were taken. Marie Nunnally sat with another cheerleader. Last week I'd nearly mustered enough courage to ask her out, but that was before she'd been given the oversized ring three days ago by a senior who no doubt awaited her arrival back at the school. And who waited for me? Nobody. No girl waited with eager arms. No girl had sat in the bleachers exulting in my baskets, suffering in our defeat. I dropped my duffel bag on the floor and took a seat beside Red Simpson. "You had yourself a good game tonight," he said.

"Thanks."

"Been a long time since we've had anybody score twenty-five points. I can name a few who did it, but it's the most anybody's scored since Coach Knight took over the team. But I'll bet it's been a real long time since we had a sophomore score that many. I don't know if it's ever been done."

"Mostly free throws," I said.

"Yeah, but you've got to hit those free throws. There's been many a game won or lost at the free-throw line. You ought to know that yourself. Those free throws you hit against South Habersham. If you'd missed them we would have gone into overtime, and maybe lost the game. I've thought about it a lot. Suppose every man on the team—subs and starters alike—all hit one more free throw per game. That would be twelve points a game more. No, it would be eleven because Graham's gone. But just think about what would happen if we scored eleven more points per game."

"Yeah."

"Say the team averaged fifty points a game. Eleven points would bring it up to over sixty."

When we finally arrived back at the school I watched Marie walk toward a car, enter it, and slide over to the middle of the front seat next to her new boyfriend. Did she kiss him? No, but she would kiss him before the night was over; why, she was practically in his lap. As the boy cranked the car and they rode from the parking lot I was overwhelmed by a wave of melancholy. "You ready, Hoard?"

"Huh?" I turned to see Gus.

"You ready to go?"

"Yeah." Why, I'd almost forgotten I was spending the night out with Gus Thompson at his grandparents' house. I followed him to a car where his older brother, Ron, sat with Truckie Myers.

"Big hero, Hoard," taunted Gus as we got in the car. "You know what we ought to do?"

"What?"

"We ought to go get us some beer. You know, to kind of celebrate your record."

"Sounds good to me."

"Take us to get some beer, Ron," said Gus. "Or else give us both one of yours."

"One of ours?" cried Truckie. "Are you accusing us of drinking beer?"

"Don't give me any of that, Truckie," Gus said. "I smell it on you right now. Now either give us one, or get us one."

Ron drove us down to the motel where Tyrone, a senior, worked as night clerk. Until the GBI had moved in, the motel had been a favorite hangout of athletes who mixed liquor into canned drinks in the back room where Tyrone slept. But with GBI agents present, and rumors leaking, Tyrone had been restricted to no more than two visitors at a time. And so, with two people in the lobby now, Gus and I scurried to the back room to share an offered drink of Coke and bourbon. We downed it quickly, returning to Ron's car. He drove past the square and beyond Rosemont's Feed and Seed, winding along a steep dirt road, turning at a crossroads, and stopping at a house. Ron left the car, walked to the carport, and knocked on a door. A light clicked on and a black man, his arms crossed, came outside and talked with Ron, shaking his head once, twice, until Ron's arm extended with an offer of cash. The man hesitated, but went back inside the house. I lay low in the seat, my heart pounding, expecting to see the GBI drive up any minute to slap handcuffs on us and haul us off to jail. If a bootlegger lived here, a raid was possible. The man stayed in the house an interminable time. A siren wailed in the distance. Why didn't the man hurry? Why didn't Ron forget the whole idea and get us out of here? Finally the man emerged and handed a paper bag to Ron, who brought it to the car and removed two cans of beer, handing one to Truckie. The other four he gave to Gus, saying, "You owe me two dollars."

"Two dollars?"

"He charged me three dollars for the six pack. It was the only way he'd sell it to me."

After an exchange of money for beer, Gus opened a can and handed it to me. "Thanks," I said and gulped down the first swallows, my lip curling at the taste. Quickly, I drained the first can and asked Gus for the second.

"Twenty-five points, huh," said Truckie. "So I guess you think you're hot stuff."

"No," I began.

"I saw Carolyn Samples do the same thing last year," he said. "Just think, Hoard, you've done just what any girl might do. Now if you'd scored twenty-five points in a football game, I'd shake your hand."

"I'd kiss your ass," said Gus's brother.

"Ron, you and Truckie leave Hoard alone. Y'all are just jealous you can't play basketball."

"Basketball, hell. We wrestle. We engage in manly sports."

"Basketball is a manly sport."

"It is? Then how come we have a girls' basketball team. You don't see us having a girls' wrestling team, do you? No, because wrestling is a manly sport."

Having finished my beers, I leaned against the door and considered that after the first few swallows, a beer drunk fast enough didn't taste half bad. I closed my eyes, the conversation fading from consciousness until suddenly I realized the car had stopped. Gus opened the door beside him and said, "Come on, Hoard."

I tried to move, but my legs failed me. Funny, but usually my legs worked when my brain told them to. It was funny enough for me to collapse on the seat and laugh.

"Damn, Gus," exclaimed Ron. "He's drunk."

"No, he ain't. He ain't had but two beers." Gus turned toward me, his face contorted in an incredulous grin, the silliest grin I'd ever seen. I pointed at him and laughed.

"Hoard, are you drunk?"

"Nooo," I replied, the word hanging in my mouth before detaching itself from my tongue and finally resonating outside my head. "Nooo," I repeated, erupting with more giggles.

"Gus, he is drunk."

"Nooo, I am not," I said. "I most certainly am not." I sat up, straightened my shirt collar and said, "I'm sober as a judge." It was one of the funniest things I'd ever said and left me collapsing with laughter again. Even Truckie thought my line hilarious.

"Gus," said Ron. "You can't take him into Pawpaw's like that."

"Listen, Hoard, listen," warned Gus, grabbing my shirt and pulling me up. "You've got to shut up now. We're fixing to go in to Pawpaw's. Can you stand up now? Can you?"

"Sure, I can. What do you think I am?" I asked, "drunk or something?" setting everyone to laughing again. I had never realized it before, but Truckie and Ron weren't such bad guys after all.

"Look, Hoard, we're going in, and you're going to have to be quiet or we'll get caught. Do you want to get caught?"

"Nooo, nooo, I don't want to get caught, Gus. Let's don't get caught."

"Alright, then you have to be quiet," Gus said, leading me from the car and through the yard. He opened the back door, leading me in to the darkened house and through the kitchen. I was clutching at his shoulder, quiet until my thigh hit the corner of a table.

"Gus?" The voice came from a dark room. "Is that you?"

"Yeah, Pawpaw. It's me."

"Somebody with you?"

"Yeah. Dickey is with me. You know I told you he was coming to spend the night."

"Who?"

"Dickey Hoard. Pawpaw, you know Dickey Hoard. He's on the basketball team with me."

"There's cornbread in there. And some pinto beans. You want anything?"

"No, Pawpaw. We stopped at the Varsity. We're going on to bed."

"Well, good night."

"Good night," said Gus, clutching his hand over my mouth. Not that I would have said anything anyway. I was afraid the words would detach themselves from my tongue and simply float away. We entered a bedroom, and I removed my blazer and tie and white shirt and finally my trousers. "Gus . . . ," I said.

"Quiet, Hoard."

"Would Tracy care if I doubled dated with y'all sometime?"

"No, she wouldn't care."

"Good. Then all I've got to do is find a date. If I'm going to double-date with y'all, then I've got to find me a date. A fellow can't double-date unless he has a date, can he?"

"That's right, Hoard. Now be quiet."

"I tell you who I wish I could go out with is Marie Nunnally."

"She's going steady."

"I know. And I can't go out with her. A fellow can't go out with another boy's steady. It just ain't right, Gus. It just ain't right. I mean if I was going steady, and somebody went out with my girl . . ."

"Hoard, go to sleep."

I lay quietly, thinking of Marie Nunnally, and suddenly I had a plan, a good plan. I'd become a great basketball player, earn scads of money and make shaving-cream commercials. Then all the girls would be sorry they had married some guy selling brushes door to door, sorry they hadn't wanted to marry me. I'd show them. I'd work hard to get better. There was no time to waste.

"Gus," I said. "Gus, wake up."

"What is it, Hoard?"

"Let's go outside and run."

"Shut up, Hoard. We're not going outside to run. Now go to sleep."

I lay thinking of how some day I would play basketball for the Atlanta Hawks, and stand around at some nightclub bar after scoring twenty-five points against the Celtics, beautiful women clinging to either arm, people clamoring for my autograph, and Tessa would approach me, dragging her worm of a husband behind her to introduce us: "Harold, this is Dickey Hoard. He and I went to school together. You played great tonight, Dickey." And I'd let her talk for a while before telling her, "Sorry, but I don't seem to remember who you are."

I giggled.

"What is it now, Hoard?" said Gus.

"I want to play basketball."

"Not now, Hoard, we've already played. You remember the game, don't you? You got twenty-five points."

"Yeah. Against the Celtics."

"The Boston Celtics? You're crazy, Hoard. Now go to sleep."

Chapter
Fourteen

On Monday morning I expected the accolades as I walked into the auditorium for morning study hall prior to homeroom. I stood behind a row of students who by now would have heard the news of my twenty-five points, either from reading the Sunday Athens newspaper or by word of mouth, and would be marveling at the achievement.

"Can you believe what he did?" exclaimed a girl wearing purple lipstick.

"No, had he ever done it before?"

Blushing, I moved forward to hear more of the conversation, staying behind the girls, "I don't think so. Least ways, not any time that I'd ever heard about. He's not even sixteen."

"Really? And he did that?"

"It was his brother's car. And when they found him driving it, and he didn't have his license . . ."

I moved away to hear other conversations: "So if you take the radius of the circle and multiply it by . . . ," "Copy your chemistry homework . . . ," "And she said he was an idiot and he turned around and said he'd only been an idiot because he was going with her and she said . . ."

The bell sounded for first period, and girls flitted by in pairs, chatting about anything but basketball. From behind me, someone grabbed my shoulder. Clarence Wilson, grinning at me, said, "Hey, I heard about what you did Saturday night." Flushing with appropriate modesty I said, "Yeah, it was mostly free—"

"You got a little bit drunk, didn't you?"

Aghast, I turned and walked away. "Don't get mad," Clarence said, following me down the corridor. "I heard all about it. I ain't going to tell. I get drunk myself. Anyway, I heard you were funny."

"Yeah, I was real funny," I said, pulling away. How many people had already heard about my sins done in the presence of three people while hearing nothing about the good done in the presence of a thousand? What a school! What people!

I passed by Truckie Myers in the hallway. He grinned at me and shook his head. Gus greeted me by lifting an imaginary can to his lips. Butch Graham saw me and invested complete attention in his girlfriend, so he wouldn't have to speak.

Even most of the references to basketball that came from those seated near me in first period focussed on Friday night. "Yeah, he went to sit up in the stands instead of with the team."

"Heck, he might could have got back in the game and helped win it. . . ."

The responses of students to my record, the feelings I had about my performance, left me perplexed. For years I had dreamed of being high scorer in a varsity basketball game. And now it had happened. And how did I feel? Elated? Successful? No, I felt it had all been a fluke. That I had to go out and prove myself all over again. I sulked as Tony drove us to the drug store for a drink before taking me home to get my practice clothes. When he pulled into our driveway, he said, "Something's wrong."

"What do you mean?"

"Look," he said, and pointed toward the back screened door where Mammie stood, her face red, her hands trembling. "Dickey," she called. "Oh, Dickey."

My stomach tightened in anticipation. Someone had been killed. No, maybe she had learned about my beers on Saturday night. "What is it?" I called out, getting out of the car and walking toward her.

"Dickey, they've done caught the men who killed your father. Five of them. And the main one was that old man, Cliff Park."

Chapter Fifteen

The State of Georgia wasted little time bringing Cliff Park and his four accomplices to justice. Within four days after news leaked of their arrests, the Grand Jury filed indictments against Park for organizing and buying my father's death, and against Park's underling, Doug Pinion, who contributed five hundred dollars and procured twenty-three-year-old Lloyd Seay to carry out the bombing. It was John Blackwell, who was hiding out at Seay's house after escaping from the Pickens County jail, who had actually planted the dynamite. But neither he nor Seay would stand trial, for they pled guilty and turned state's evidence in exchange for life sentences. The fifth conspirator, Iris Worley, who had driven Blackwell and Seay to South Carolina to buy dynamite, would elude the law until after Park's trial had begun on January 2.

The first morning of the trial the two sides selected a jury from 127 people. For hours, Nat Hancock, a Jefferson attorney, had stood near the judge's bench chanting 127 times something too fast and garbled for me to decipher, while Cliff Park sat beside his attorneys, Horace Wood and Wesley Asinof, a lawyer from Atlanta. When Park wasn't smiling and waving at people in the courtroom, or turning to whisper something to his lawyer after one of Nat's outbursts, he was fingering the brim of his gray Stetson, absently hooking his lower plate over his upper lip and popping his teeth from his mouth. He appeared as bored with the monotony of the proceedings as I was.

"How long will this go on?" I asked Mama during a recess.

"They're halfway done," she said, which I took as an encouragement for me to leave. I returned on the second morning in time to hear the state make it's charge: "That Floyd Hoard was bombed to death because he dared to interfere with Park's bootlegging in this county, and that Cliff Park was not actually present at the bombing, but he did cause it, procure it, aide and abet it." He would be given no recommendation of mercy. The parade of witnesses began with Albert, Horace Jackson, and Peggy Jean. I had been excluded, though Mama had asked me shortly before Christmas, "Do you want to be subpoenaed?" Mortified, I had told her, "absolutely not," before asking, "What's subpoenaed?"

"Do you want to testify in court?"

"What'll they ask me?"

"They'll ask what you saw that morning," she said, her chin lifted in an effort at self-control, which I knew would collapse at the first mention of Daddy's name. Her eyes were already welling with tears.

"No," I told her, feeling the anger rise within me. I wanted no public reliving of that morning. Not that I hadn't silently relived it again and again, but I couldn't risk a display of tears before a courtroom full of spectators and have my grief documented by newspapers.

Peggy Jean agreed to testify, but had answered only a few questions before Asinof asked the judge to spare her any more anxiety. Judge Dunahoo refused, and Peggy Jean sat with her fists clenched and her eyes staring at nothing in an effort to keep her composure. "Well, I don't know how I got outside. I ran, I know. The car was in the front yard. Well, you could see a tire to the right side, and it was just a mass of metal. That's what it appeared to me. And Daddy had been thrown into the back seat, and his legs were over the front seat, and the dash was—." She had halted, putting her hands to her face before continuing, "the midsection of his body—and it seemed to me that he was breathing when I first got out to him, but after a couple of minutes—"

"Did you do anything for him?"

I caught my breath, waiting for her to tell of instructing me to do mouth-to-nose. "Well," she said, "I had a course in first aid, and I felt for his pulse, but I couldn't find it, and when he stopped breathing, I tried mouth-to-nose resuscitation to get him back to breathing, but I never did."

"Your witness."

"No questions."

And that was it. "What?" I thought. "What about me? What does everybody think I was doing that morning? Standing around blubbering like some child? The papers the next morning told the story of the "attractive and heroic sixteen-year-old daughter" who tried to save her father's life, a story that took longer to read than it had taken Peggy Jean to testify, and though I never mentioned the incident to Peggy Jean, I remained piqued at being overlooked, as if I didn't know the taste of charred flesh.

Ronnie Angel followed, telling of buying beer and whiskey from Park and of the ensuing raid. Another man testified that Doug Pinion had been an employee of Park. Billy Elder, the clerk of court, testified about padlock proceedings on Park's establishment. Most of the trial was boring. Even the testimony of one of the conspirators had been dry. I had been present when John Blackwell first entered the courtroom to swear on the Bible and slump into the witness chair. He was twenty-four-years old, had black hair and a forehead too big for the rest of his face, sleepy eyelids, and a bad cold. At least he talked as if he had a bad cold; his words were nasal and drawled slowly as he told of his escape from jail, his hiding out at the residence of Lloyd Seay, and the day Seay first asked him if he "had the nerve to kill a man."

"What did you say to that?" came the question from the prosecuting attorney, Luther Hames.

"I told him I didn't."

"Where did this conversation take place?"

"At his home."

"Did you subsequently or any time thereafter have any conversation that related back to this conversation that you had in his home?"

"Well, he brought it up later on. Couple of weeks, I guess, about killing a man."

"And what was the conversation then?"

"Would I help him blow that man up."

"Did he tell you who was to be blown up?"

"No, he didn't."

"Now, at the time that you were having any conversations with him about it, do you know whether or not he made any telephone call?"

"He made one the day we went to South Carolina."

"And do you recall what day you went to South Carolina?"

"I believe it was a Thursday."

"Do you recall with reference to the Thursday before or the Thursday after the death of Floyd Hoard?"

"Before."

"And do you know who he called?"

"No, I don't."

"And after he called, what did you do?"

"He hung up the phone and said, 'let's go'."

"And where did you go?"

"We come to a restaurant on the—"

"Do you know the name of the restaurant?"

"I do now. It's Blue Bird Truck Stop."

"And what highway was it on?

"Eighty-five."

"And what did you do when you got to the restaurant?"

"We met the man that I found out is Iris Worley."

"Now, how long were you there at the restaurant?"

"About twenty-five minutes, I imagine."

"Did you go inside?"

"Yes."

"Did anyone else go inside with you?"

"Lloyd."

"When you say Lloyd, who is Lloyd?"

"Seay."

"What did you have to eat there?"

"I eat a steak and he eat soup, I believe it was."

"Did anything happen before you finished your meal?"

"Yes, a man pulled through the parking lot and Lloyd said, 'Let's go, that's the man'."

"What color car were you traveling in at that time?"

"Blue and white '58 Ford."

"And what color car was the man traveling in who came to the parking lot?"

"It was a white Chrysler."

"Which car did you go in?"

"The white Chrysler."

"And where did you go?"

"South Carolina."

"Was there any conversation in the car en route to South Carolina?"

"Worley said that he knowed somebody that he could buy some dynamite from."

"Was there any question about who was to make the purchase of the dynamite?"

"No."

"Who did make the purchase?"

"When we got there, he told me to go in and get it."

"Who told you to go in and get it?"

"Lloyd, I believe it was."

And so it went, Blackwell telling of how he had purchased ten sticks of dynamite and on the following Sunday afternoon drank beer and swallowed pills before riding to Worley's house. Shortly after midnight, he, Worley, and Seay drove past our house. Seay told Blackwell to get out and walk into the yard and make sure there was a '65 Ford with a radio pole on it. After checking in our yard, he walked back to a dirt road, where he told Seay and Worley the car wasn't there. They had reckoned that perhaps Floyd Hoard had traded cars, and sent Blackwell back into our yard to wire the dynamite despite their uncertainty. Creeping in the shadows, hearing our dogs barking off in the distance, he raised the hood and wired the dynamite "up towards the front, close to the front."

"Up towards the front. How far from where you had attached the ground wire did you lay the dynamite?" By then, it was Asinof cross-examining the witness.

"I don't know how far it was."

"Well, you don't remember?"

"No, I couldn't say."

"Mister Blackwell, what affect did those pills that you had give you?"

"They just—I don't know what they hardly do to you."

"Well, did you feel sleepy? Did you feel wide awake? Did you feel like you could jump through a ten-story window and walk out of it?"

"Yes, that's about the way it makes you feel."

"You felt pretty big?"

"I don't know if I felt big or not."

"I mean you felt that you could do almost anything. Is that right?"

"Yes."

"I am trying to find out how you felt at that time after taking those pills on that date."

"I felt crazy. Wild like."

"You felt crazy. Wild like?"

"What effect does it have when you take beer with it?"

"It just peps them up."

From the balcony, I stared down at John Blackwell, loathing him. Out of his mind on drugs and alcohol, this man, who had never set dynamite in his life, who, as one expert testified, could have been blown-up himself if he had set the dynamite to the wrong wire, had managed to come into our yard and do the impossible. If there was a God, I reasoned, He would have let the killer be killed, not my father. God would have sent a rabbit off in the woods or the ghost of Tommy Winters to drift past for the dogs to go chasing, would have waked Daddy or someone up to see the hood raised in the yard and the man bending over with the dynamite, or maybe would have kept a prison guard alert to prevent John Blackwell's escape, would have had Park or Pinion or Seay, all bootleggers, or Worley, a convicted car thief, arrested before the murder. Every one of them should have been in jail. If only one of them had been locked up, the entire plan may have broken down, and there would have been no murder. Wouldn't that have been easy enough for God to do?

"Just plain mean," Mammie had said later that evening at supper. "Dickey, that Blackwell man had no idea whose car he was setting that dynamite to. They said he didn't even know your Daddy."

"I was there," I said curtly. "I heard it all."

"Dickey, it could have been the wrong house. He was so drunk and doped up he didn't care whose house it was. It could just as easily been you or your mama or your little sisters in that car. Lord, he didn't care. He's just plain mean."

"No, he ain't mean," I said.

"Well you know he is."

"No," I thought. Considering that Blackwell had actually committed the murder, yet received only fifteen hundred dollars while Seay and Worley each kept two thousand dollars for telling Blackwell what to do, I thought he must have been pretty stupid. He did only what somebody told him to do and never asked, "Why?" He just did it. Seay said get in the car, and he did. Seay and Worley said buy dynamite, and he did. They said set this bomb, and he did. He just obeyed.

"No, Mammie," I said. "I think he's more stupid than mean."

"Well, of course, he's stupid, but you know he's mean, too."

"I reckon."

"Are you going back down there tomorrow, Doll-boy?"

"No, I'm going on to school." Though the principal, Miss Blackstock, had offered me an excused absence for any day of the trial, I had attended at least half a day of school each day to be counted present and eligible for basketball practice. And though Coach Knight had been sympathetic, telling me "if you need to miss practice, Dickey, just let me know," now that I was in the starting lineup I intended to stay there. I told him I'd be at practice.

Two mornings later, a Saturday morning, a wind chilled the courthouse yards, where a few men wearing the white uniforms with the blue stripe that identified them as inmates from the county farm worked on the grounds, stopping to discuss the identity of anyone coming up the steps. Inside, the courthouse smelled of stale tobacco. Men in suits stood by the Coke machine, men in overalls smoked cigarettes by the space heaters, which looked like steel accordions, discussing the case while taking swigs from drink bottles, clearing throats and spitting wads of brown mucous toward the wide mouths of spittoons. Some of them eyed me curiously as I walked down the gray corridor and up the wooden stairs toward Nat Hancock's office, where I found my Aunt Claudine reclining against her desk. "Well, hello, Dickey," she said. "Heard y'all won the game last night."

"Yeah," I said, thankful we'd won our first game of the Holiday Tournament, which meant that we wouldn't have to play Commerce tonight. Earlier in the year some of their students had devised a cheer for me, "One, two, three, BOOM. You ain't got no father. One, two, three, BOOM. . . ."

"How many did you get?" she asked, winking at our inside joke—she knew good and well that I kept a running count of my points, just like Al used to do when he played.

"Thirteen," I said, blushing at the other female presence in the room.

"Albert said he thought you probably had about that many. Can I get you a Coke, Dickey?" I nodded affirmatively. "This is Tillie Gayton," Claudine said, acknowledging the girl, or was she a woman? Her red and swollen eyes made it hard for me to tell her age. She held a Coke bottle in one hand, a cigarette in the other, her lips curled in a troubled frown.

"Tillie, this is my nephew, Dickey. He's Fuzzy's son. He's on the high school basketball team." I extended my hand and said, "Pleased to meet you, Miss Gayton."

She didn't look at me, but she almost smiled. "Tillie," she said. "Just Tillie."

"Tillie testified last night," Claudine said. "She wants everyone to know what happened because she wants to do what's right. We're all so proud of her for wanting to get her life back together. She has done the right thing." Putting her arm on Tillie's shoulder, she said, "And life is going to be better for you from now on."

Claudine left to get my Coke. I sat uneasily, staring mostly at my feet, wondering why the woman had been called to testify. She lit a cigarette and asked me, "So how old are you anyway?"

"Fifteen."

"Fifteen," she said, taking a long draw. "Honey, enjoy it."

"What do you mean?"

"I mean just that. Enjoy it. You're only fifteen once. I wished to God I was fifteen again and had it to do all over. Things get complicated when you get older. Believe me. You'll see." She said nothing more until Claudine returned with the Coke. I nervously sipped from the bottle, and to my relief, Tillie left the room.

"Who is she, anyway?" I asked.

Claudine whispered that Tillie was John Blackwell's girlfriend. "Oh," I said, nodding in recognition. She was the woman who had lived in South Georgia with Blackwell from August until November. The still they were operating in the basement of a rented house blew up and they were arrested for arson. A few days later, the owner went knocking on the door of the Johnson County sheriff, Roland Attaway, saying he suspected that Blackwell knew something about the Hoard murder. He and another man, Lloyd Seay, were always reading newspaper accounts about it and discussing it and one day Blackwell had let slip, "You're not the one who set the dynamite."

Sheriff Attaway hounded the two men for a confession, and escorted Tillie to the Fulton County jail in Atlanta, where Blackwell had been held after his recapture. Tillie testified that she had told Blackwell, "nobody has a right to take a man's life but God," and "if you know anything about it, you should tell." Blackwell signed a confession, opening the door for Seay's arrest, and upon Seay's confession and collaborating evidence, Worley's, Pinion's, and Park's arrests as well.

"How old is she?"

"Twenty. And you know, Dickey, she seems real smart. You just wonder how somebody like her could get mixed up with somebody like Blackwell. People sure get themselves in messes with the company they keep."

The door to the courtroom opened and Nat Hancock entered, greeting me. He had known me all my life and had always been friendly. "Mister Hancock," I said. "I've been meaning to ask you something."

"What's that?"

"The first day of all this you were standing up in front of the courtroom saying something for the life of me I couldn't figure out."

"Are you talking about when we were sequestering the jurors?"

"I don't know. Whatever it was you were saying, you were saying real fast. 'Juror-da-da-DA-da-something-something-juror.'"

"Oh, I was saying, "Juror, look upon the plaintiff, plaintiff look upon the juror."

"What does it mean?"

"It means that the state which is prosecuting Mister Park is given its opportunity to either strike a juror or say that the juror is cleared for duty. For instance, the juror can look to the state and say, 'I'm opposed to capital punishment and the state which is seeking the death penalty can say, 'We think this person should be struck from the jury.' Then later I was saying, 'Juror look upon the defendant, defendant look upon the juror,' and Mister Park had his opportunity to say, 'I think this person would be a fair choice to serve on the jury.' For instance, they struck one juror because he was some distant kin to your mother. And the state struck some jurors as well. We are just trying to let Mister Park have a fair trial. You believe he ought to get a fair trial, don't you, Dickey?"

"Yes, sir," I said, shaking my head in confusion. "But, Mister Hancock . . ."

"Yeah," he said, waiting. All I could do was shake my head, not knowing how to ask my next question. How could these five men be innocent if the state had already found enough evidence to arrest them? How could these jurors, people like Runt Moore and Tessa Halley's father, understand enough about the law to judge

Cliff Park? How could anyone get a fair trial when everybody in my school already had their minds made up as soon as the arrests were made? "No, he couldn't have done it?" some said. "I'm not surprised. Figured it all along," said others before the case even entered the courtroom.

"Oh, nothing," I said, finishing my drink and standing to leave by the same route I'd entered, down the back stairwell because court was already in session. "Dickey, you may want to stay around this morning. Seay has been testifying," Claudine said.

Shutting the door behind me, I turned to see Tillie Gayton gazing out the window, smoking another cigarette, never looking toward me. I started to speak, but thought better of it and walked quietly down the stairs, down the corridor and turned the corner to climb the balcony steps and sit on a folded chair near a few black men who looked down on the courtroom.

Mama sat where she had sat all week, in a wood chair at a table littered with Coke bottles and cracker wrappers beneath the fan suspended from the high ceiling marred by water stains. Beside her sat the team of attorneys, Colonel Davis and Wes Channel, the new solicitor appointed to replace Daddy, and Luther Hames, the chief prosecuting attorney for the state. Across the room sat Asinof and Horace Wood, and the old man who sat popping his lower plate from his mouth.

Seay, a pallid man with squinting eyes, sat surveying the courtroom, his eyes remaining alert as Luther Hames questioned him, his testimony provoking frequent outbursts from Park's lawyer, who objected "to anything the witness 'guessed,'" or "to any conversation the witness had out of the presence of the defendant." After a series of objections, Luther Hames had glared at Asinof before turning to the stenographer and saying, "Miss Reporter, would you read me the questions back. I have been interrupted so many times, I don't know just exactly what my train of thought was."

The reporter, long motionless except for the continuous movement of fingers on the keys of her machine, lifted up a long strip of paper and read: "Question: And when you were dealing with Mister

Park, or was Doug Pinion the only one you ever dealt with in behalf of Park? Answer: Yes, sir, he was. Question: Then you knew that they had this conversation with him in June."

Luther Hames nodded his appreciation at the reporter and turned again toward Seay. "Then you knew when you were dealing with Doug Pinion in June that you were dealing with him as the agent of Mister Park?"

"Yes, sir."

"Now—"

Asinof was again on his feet. "We move to exclude that answer, Your Honor, and object to the question on the grounds it calls for a conclusion."

"Let me ask you this," Mr. Hames's voice was raised in agitation, "Did you know that based upon the type of dealings that you had with Doug Pinion and Mister Park over a period of three years—"

"We object to that as calling for a conclusion."

"No, sir," Hames argued. "It doesn't call for a conclusion. What led him to that conclusion?"

"I agree with that," said Judge Dunahoo, leaning back in his chair. "I will overrule it."

"I say—you knew at the time you began this conversation with Doug Pinion on the eleventh day of June that he was acting on behalf of A. C. "Cliff" Park?"

"Yes, sir."

"And how did he describe A. C. Park?"

"The 'Old Man'."

"Have you had other conversations with Doug Pinion in which he referred to A. C. "Cliff" Park as the 'Old Man'?"

"Yes, sir," replied Seay. "I have."

"Was that the way—state whether or not that was the way he had always described to you A. C. "Cliff" Park."

"Yes, sir, he always called him 'the old man'."

"During any of the conversations did he tell you that Solicitor Hoard had cost A. C. "Cliff" Park a lot of money?"

"I don't remember whether he said Solicitor Hoard did or not. He did tell me about the raid up there. They got a lot of beer and stuff from Mister Park."

"Did he tell you why he wanted him killed?"

"No, sir, he didn't."

"What sum of money did he offer you for the purpose of killing Solicitor Hoard?"

"Five thousand dollars, the first time."

"Now, at that time, what discussion was had relative to how the killing was to be accomplished? As to what means, whether it was a gun, dynamite, or what else?"

"Pinion stated that it would be best just to take a shotgun and drive up—he told me what time the solicitor came home every day, by himself at a certain time—and it would be best just to ride by and kill him with a shotgun on the road."

Why hadn't he tried that, I thought? My father would have had his chance to survive, maybe looked in his rearview mirror to see a car speeding up behind him. Daddy kept a pistol, was a good shot, had one day shot a snake out of the top of an oak tree; he could have gunned down Seay and Blackwell both, or at least had time to call for help by his car radio.

"I wasn't interested," continued Seay. "Then when he asked me about it two or three more times, I told him I would check around for him and see if anybody wanted to do it."

"Did you talk to anyone about it?"

"Yes, sir, I first talked to—well, I talked to several people about it. Iris Worley was about the third or fourth. I just had a habit of mentioning it to anybody I seen, because I didn't take him too seriously on the subject."

"When you talked to Iris Worley, what did he have to say about whether or not he was interested?"

"Sir, he wanted to do it."

"Which Iris Worley are you talking about?"

"The one that lives in Commerce. The one indicted in this case."

"Did you tell him what he could get if he killed Solicitor Hoard?"

"Yes, sir. I told him it was five thousand dollars."

"What, if anything, did Iris Worley say as to whether or not he would do it for five thousand dollars?"

"He said he would do it, but that he thought he ought to have seventy-five hundred, and asked me to go back and tell the party. He didn't know who I was talking about, but he asked me to go back and tell him, and I did."

"Who did you go back to?"

"Pinion."

"Did you tell him that you had somebody that would do it for more money?"

"Yes, sir. I had told him that I had saw somebody, but they wanted seventy-five hundred instead of five thousand."

"What did Doug Pinion say?"

"He said, 'Well, that is all the man will pay.' No, at first he said, 'I don't think the man will pay any more. I will go see.'"

"Did he later contact you about it?"

"I think that was the time he had me to wait while he said he would go see."

"And how long did you wait?"

"I couldn't say for sure. I'd say approximately forty-five minutes or an hour."

"Where were you at that time?"

"At Pinion's house."

"In Jackson County?"

"Yes, sir."

"Doug Pinion, himself, added five hundred dollars to the price on Floyd Hoard's death?"

"Yes, sir."

"Did you have any conversation with Worley about whether or not you wanted to withdraw from this matter?"

"Yes, sir. I told him from the beginning that I didn't want to be implicated in it."

"After you had purchased the dynamite, or after the dynamite had been purchased, did you have a further conversation with Iris Worley to the effect that you did not want to participate?"

"Yes, sir. When he asked me to bring Blackwell down there, I told him I would bring Blackwell down there, but that was it. If they wanted to go ahead with it, they could. I just didn't want any part of it."

"Iris Worley tell you anything about what the old man would do if you withdrew from it?"

"Your Honor," shouted Asinof, leaping to his feet. "I want to object to that question on the ground that it calls for an answer which is hearsay."

"Alright, sir," Judge Dunahoo said. "Same ruling."

"Did Iris Worley tell you what the old man would do if you withdrew from it?"

"Yes, sir," said Seay. "He made a long statement about it. It's hard for me to put into words. He led me to believe that if I didn't go through with it, didn't go along with it and help him, that they, the old man, would only get someone else to do it, and I'd be the only one that knew about it other than them."

"If Your Honor please," said Asinof. "I would like the record to show at this time we are objecting and that the objections made are continuing and it is made on the same grounds as the previous objection made to this testimony."

As the lawyers debated for several minutes, Lloyd Seay studied his fingernails. So, he didn't want my father killed? Well, if he had kept his mouth shut about it, instead of talking to God-only-knew-who-all, the plot would have died instead of my father. But he had kept bringing it up. How many people had he told? How many people had become conspirators by their silence? Seay hadn't minded driving a hundred miles one way to buy dynamite, hadn't minded driving Blackwell to our house, certainly hadn't minded pocketing two thousand dollars. What he minded was being implicated. If he had feared for his wife and child, I could understand that. If he had thrown the two thousand dollars back in Pinion's face I might have believed him. But he had kept the money. To get on the witness stand now and say, "I didn't want any part of it," was an outright lie. Blackwell may have been stupid, blindly obeying any order. But this man was worse. He was a coward and a liar. And it was because he was a coward and a liar that he became a killer.

Chapter
Sixteen

Saturday night the sleet began falling and by Sunday much of Georgia had been hit by an ice storm. School was canceled Monday, but the ice didn't keep people from the courthouse, for Cliff Park was expected to take the stand. I opened the back door of the court room. "Ain't no use looking in there, son," said a man in the hallway. "Nobody's leaving their seats today." And so I tried the balcony, finding an open space between two folding chairs and sitting on the concrete floor. Below me, spectators stretched and mumbled while protecting their chairs.

Judge Dunahoo quietly entered the chambers, "All rise," said the bailiff, and the judge took his seat and tapped his gavel on a block of wood. "Alright, sir," he said to Asinof. "You may proceed."

"At this time I would like to call Mister Park to the stand, Your Honor, if you please. I would like to instruct Mister Park as his counsel."

"Alright, sir."

"Take the stand, Mister Park."

The old man rose and walked to the witness chair, tugging at his red suspenders, nodding and smiling at the jury. He sat facing his attorney, who told him, "Mister Park, you are the defendant in this case. You have been indicted by the Grand Jury of Jackson County on a charge of murder. You have entered your plea of not guilty to this charge. At this time you have the right to make to the court and to the jury such statement in your own defense as you shall see fit. They may believe it in whole or in part. They may believe it in preference to the sworn testimony in this case. So if you choose to make this statement to the jury, I suggest that you turn to the jury and that you speak out loudly and clearly and take your time, and make whatever statement in your own defense as you see fit."

Park swiveled the chair toward the jury, cleared his throat, and said, "Well, ladies and gentlemen of the jury," which I thought was funny, because there was only one woman on the jury. "On August the seventh, when we heard about Mister Hoard's murder, we was greatly shocked, my wife, myself, and my daughter. We all thought lots of Mister Hoard, as my daughter thought lots of him. He filled out her income papers, the first little income paper she had filled, and we all thought lots of him, and it was an awful shock to us, and we regretted it awful bad. But ladies and gentlemen of the jury, I didn't have one thing to do with any of it. I don't know anything about it. And I am flatly denying the whole thing, and ladies and gentlemen of the jury, I am not guilty."

He paused and for a moment it appeared he had finished. I snorted. He thought a brisk denial would save him from the chair? He'd better say more than that. He did, having paused merely to clear his throat again. "I've got a little more stuff here that I want to go over with you. Mister Hoard and I had been friends for fifteen years. He done the majority of my law business, what little I done here. He filled out my income papers. And along through the years, I sell a right smart little land. And he drawed my deeds, and he drawed my notes, and he done the principal part of my law business, and me and him got along fine. We never had a cross word."

"Mister Cliff," interrupted Judge Dunahoo, and I suddenly realized what a strain it had been to hear the old man's words above the grinding gears of a transfer truck struggling to climb the icy hill beside the courthouse. "Wait just a minute until this truck gets by, please sir, so that we can hear."

Judge Dunahoo poured himself a glass of water, Cliff Park stared at his knees, the spectators seemed to take a collective breath, as if for a minute remembering who they were, not characters in a high drama but common people watching a man now smiling at his wife and attorneys as if to ask, "Are my suspenders straight?" But when the truck passed, the old man's smile faded and he became again the indicted murderer.

"Back about ten years ago, Mister Hoard put up a little business right over here," he said, pointing with his thumb to where the old law office stood. "A little place to sell baby clothes, I think it was mostly. 'Lad and Lassie Shop.' And he didn't quite have enough money to put it up, and me and my wife lent him a thousand dollars to go ahead and put this little business up. We tried to help him. And we did help him. However, he paid me back. He didn't owe me a dime when he died. Paid me back. And we got along fine, and like I said, we never had a cross word, and he was a man I could talk to."

"And it rocked on until they made that raid, and they made some cases against me for having some beer and tax-paid whiskey, and I don't remember the date, but it was sometime after the raid and everything, and I come down there and talked with Mister Hoard, and when I went in, there was somebody in there, a Miss Wier, and I asked her if Mister Hoard was in, and she said, 'yes, have a seat, Mister Park.' Said, 'he will be through in a little bit.' "

"Well, in a few minutes, Mister I. W. Davis come out, and I spoke to Mister Hoard and told him that if he had time I would like to talk with him. And he just looked around at me and says, 'well, I'll take time to talk with you most any time. You just come on in.' And we went in his office and shut the door, and I told him what I wanted. I told him I wanted to get them cases settled. I was through with it; that my wife and daughter wanted me to get out of it, and I just wanted to get them settled, and I says, 'Mister Hoard, I want you to be reasonable,' and he looked around at me again and says, 'well, you thought that I would be reasonable with you, didn't you?' And I says, 'yes, sir, I thought you would.' "

"And Mister Hoard asked me, says, 'Mister Park, if you want to get out of it and get shut of it, what about just pulling down that case you've got to recover that beer, and I'll be reasonable,' and I says, 'Alright, sir.'"

"And so my lawyer went in, and they made the arrangements, and when the time come, we went down, and Mister Hoard was just as nice as he could be. He presented the cases, and I pleaded guilty, and that's all Mister Hoard done. And the judge put the fine on me, and I paid it, and we pulled the case down when we found what the fine would be. And he was just as nice to me as he could be, and like I said, he always had been. He'd always been nice to me."

"And this Blackwell boy that is into this. I don't know him. I never have seen him until he come in here to court that day. That's the only time I've ever seen him. And Lloyd Seay? His folks used to live in Commerce when he was a small child. I think he was about six or seven years old when they sold out and left from there and went back to Dawson or Lumpkin County, somewhere up there where they come from, and I didn't see Lloyd Seay very much, and I never had one thing to do with it at all. Not one thing in the world, and I hadn't seen him in three years until they brought him out here and put him on the stand."

"And Mister Iris Worley? I used to know Iris Worley. Just know him is all. I never had any dealings with him. No kind of way, shape, form, or fashion. And I don't know whether he would walk up here today whether I would know him or not. It's been six or eight years to my best recollection since I seen Iris Worley, and ladies and gentlemen of the jury, I was born in the house where I live now, and I lived there all my life. And there's another thing about Mister Hoard that I didn't mention while ago." He removed from his pocket a sheet of paper that he held up so that the jury could see. "I gave Mister Hoard the power of attorney in 1957. And this here is just a copy of some insurance to show that I lent Mister Hoard the money. It's got, 'Mister and Misses Floyd Hoard' on it. 'Lad and Lassie Shop. One thousand dollars.'"

"And ladies and gentlemen of the jury, God in heaven knows that I didn't have one thing in the world to do with this. I wouldn't have mistreated Mister Hoard or his family in any kind of way. We always been good friends. We never had a cross word. We worked things out. He would sit down and talk with me and work things out. And God in heaven knows that I didn't have one thing in the world to do with it in no form, shape, nor fashion. I give nobody no money. And I had nothing to do with it. And ladies and gentlemen of the jury, I am not guilty."

His attorney told him to please come down from the stand and told the court that the defense was resting its case. Because it was almost noon, I left for school, figuring that by the time I arrived home from basketball practice, the jury would have reached its verdict. They either had to say he was guilty or call the entire GBI a bunch of liars.

But by nightfall they had not reached a verdict. "He stood up there and offered evidence," Mama said, "and so the state has the right to refute it." The next morning Albert and Mrs. Wier took the stand to claim that Daddy had never considered himself and Park to be "best of friends," Asinof ranting that such testimony was hearsay and not admissible. Not until the next afternoon did the jury return its verdict, that A. C. "Cliff" Park was guilty of first degree murder and that his sentence was death in the electric chair.

Chapter
Seventeen

Of the five men convicted, only Cliff Park received the death sentence. The rest were given life. Doug Pinion would serve nearly twenty years before being paroled. Dot, Albert's sister-in-law, saw him in a restaurant shortly before he died. "My nerves is shot," he told her. Within a few weeks he was found dead in his burned-out car. Lloyd Seay also died violently, gunned down in Atlanta nearly a quarter century after the trial. John Blackwell served more than fourteen years in prison. So did Iris Worley. His daughter and I have had coffee together. She insisted she could account for her father's whereabouts the night before the murder. After his release he found work in a reputable store. As for Cliff Park, he died several years after I visited him in the hospital. I went to the funeral home to offer my condolences to his wife and daughter. Even after his death, Mrs. Park told me, "You know Cliff didn't have nothing to do with that."

The best reply I could give her was, "I don't know." Of course, by law all five men were guilty of conspiracy. But to say that Cliff Park was responsible for the death of my father is a little bit like saying that Pontius Pilate was responsible for the death of Jesus. Or to say that John Blackwell was the one who really killed him is like putting all the blame on a Roman centurion. It took a team of men, Seay, Worley, and Pinion included, pressuring and threatening and bragging and bullying, to commit the murder. Remove any one of them from the plot, and it may have never happened.

The summer brought changes. My best friends, Tony and Marcus, graduated, leaving me with knowledge that I must endure the next cross-country season without them. The anniversary of my father's death brought fresh outbursts of grief from my mother, and silent anger within me. My hopes of the summer being a time of languishing face down on a towel by the pool, diving into the blue water to dunk and show off and try to gain the attention of girls, and of joining a softball team, had been ruined back in the spring when Mama told me I needed a job.

"I've spent the whole year in school," I complained. "I don't want to spend the whole summer at some job."

"Surely by now you must have some idea about what you'd like to do for a living. Peggy Jean is a candy-striper so she can get a head start on being a doctor. You must be interested in something."

"Well, yeah, I am," I said. "I want to be a sportscaster. You know, like Milo Hamilton." It was a response that would silence her for a while, I reckoned. For what chance did she have of finding me a job around Jefferson describing Hank Aaron home runs. But to my surprise, when I got home from school the next afternoon she told me to get in the car. She drove me the nine miles to Commerce, parking in a lot outside a brick building bearing the sign WJJC.

"What is this place?"

"It's the radio station."

"Commerce has a radio station?"

"Yes," she said, "and by all means don't let this man think that you didn't know that."

She took me inside and introduced me to the owner, and before I realized what had happened, she had committed my future to the radio business. The next afternoon my training began by observing a blind man play records and a sixteen-year-old boy write down readings from the transmitter meters, tear off news stories from the United Press International wire (which ran constantly outside the rest room), insert tapes in machines, and during network newscasts dub tapes. They seemed pleased to have me as an audience for their knowledge and a subject for their derision. They told me that the Federal Communications Commission could be listening at any time to monitor for superfluous language, and so I had best take care what I said, that the station could be sued if I read anything from the wire service containing a defamation, and that the last trainee had been fired for remarks spoken while unaware that a microphone had been left "open."

Every weekday and Saturday I reported for work. My only break during the day was a trip to the store for honey buns and chocolate milk for my teachers, the trips consuming more and more time as each day passed, until finally one of my mentors complained: "An hour for a trip to buy a honey bun! What are you doing up there? Reading all their magazines?"

By July I had taken and passed a test for my broadcasting license and had been allotted a half hour on the air each evening. And so my summer passed, seven-and-a-half hours a day of observing, thirty minutes of air time, and not a dollar to show for it. To my shy request for a small salary the station owner told me a story of how Milo Hamilton got his start announcing Ohio State football games and never asking for a dime. I had nodded politely until he finished his story, waiting for his answer, before realizing that his story had been meant as a negative reply. And so I remained penniless, nervous, and bored.

My deliverance came late in mid-July when my Aunt Lanelle telephoned and told Mama that Calder had more peaches in his orchard than he could pick and that he could sure use my help. Gladly I consented. I was bored enough to have accepted a tour of duty in Vietnam. By the next morning I was on a bus headed to Calder's, where during summers past I had whiled away afternoons eating peanuts and drinking Cokes as Calder plotted his checker strategies and distracted my own by singing, "Going to king in Texas now," or, "I got a gal, a bulldog, too, the gal don't love me but the bulldog do." Or I played army with Ricky Lister and several of the local black children, Bo-dilly, Alvin, and Milton, fighting imaginary Nazis in the woods and pastures surrounding the store. Often we played baseball with a rubber ball and the oak stick that Calder used to secure the store's sliding wooden door at night.

Two years had passed since my last summer visit, and I quickly learned that much had changed, even at Calder's. Most of my black playmates had left home, and anyway, at fifteen, I would have felt silly playing army, and the baseball sandlot seemed to have shrunk. Nothing was the same. "Mama and Daddy are expecting you to work," warned my cousin Sara upon my arrival at the bus station. "They haven't called you to come down here and play. And I sure hope you don't think you're gonna sit around at the store all day long drinking Co-colas."

"No," I sighed, laying my suitcase in the trunk of the car. I didn't think I was going to play at all; adults had all but eliminated the word "play" from my vocabulary.

She had not yet finished her lecture. "You'll have to sleep with Ken in my room. He hasn't even gone home at night. He and Daddy get up at the crack of dawn and they don't come home till dark. I know they're all about worn out. They need you to help them."

Ken was Sara's boyfriend, a quiet and surly young man who had graduated with honors from high school in June. He was a bookworm who I'd never spent much time with, and who when he was led captive by Sara to our house on Thanksgiving or Christmas, would seldom string together more than two words at a time for my benefit. Prospects of sharing a room with him for a few weeks promised some awkward exchanges.

Neither Ken nor Calder were at the house when we arrived. "Lord, Hon," cried Lanelle as she set two sandwiches before me at the kitchen table. "Sara's gonna have to take Calder his lunch at the store, and Ken's to the orchard. I tell you we haven't even had time to sit down to eat around here the past two weeks. The peaches are going to rot on the trees if we don't get them picked. Sara will run you down to the store when she takes Calder's lunch."

After finishing my sandwiches I rode with Sara to the wood building where my uncle sold soft drinks and candy, milk and bread, potted meat, sardines and crackers, dungarees and work gloves, watermelon from his fields and an abundance of peaches. "Hey, Dickey-boy," he said when I entered. "How you been, Dickey-boy. You ready to go to work for me? I sho need ya, ya heah. I got some peaches now, ya heah?"

"That's what I've heard," I said. "What you want me to do?"

"I want you to tend this sto' while I check on Ken, ya heah?" he said, the right corner of his upper lip twitching when he ended his sentence. "Come out heah a minute." He motioned for me to follow him to a flat-bed truck parked near the highway. "These peaches in this basket is twenty-five cents. These bigger baskets heah is thirty-five. These heah is fifty. Tell 'em to come to the orchard and pick their own for seventy-five cents a bushel. A dollar a bushel if we pick 'em."

"All right," I said, watching as Calder cranked his '52 pickup truck and drove away. I breathed a sigh of relief. Sara had made the work sound worse than it was. Walking inside the store, I opened a Nehi Grape, savoring its flavor, my only interruptions coming from a man who bought a fifty-cent basket of peaches and from two black children who bought soft drinks and a small sack of penny candy. When they left, I cooled off by lying on top of the drink box for about a half hour until Calder returned and told me to go to the orchard. "Drive my truck up there and let Ken get home. He ain't been home in two days and he say he needs some mo' clothes. You know how to drive, don't ya?"

"Sure, I can drive. Joe used to let me drive all the time."

"You got a license?"

I frowned and said, "A learner's license," expecting Calder to retract his offer of the truck. But he surprised me by saying, "Be careful driving on that highway, ya heah."

"All right," I said, grinning, grateful to be treated like a man, quite a change from the way Mama and Mammie treated me. I drove the truck along the highway for about a quarter mile and turned through the orchard gate and found Ken sitting beneath a peach tree. Beside him was a cardboard box top serving as a makeshift sign—"Peaches,

Pick your Own 75¢ a Bushel"—and a metal box emptied of its fishing tackle and filled with cash. Ken wore a white t-shirt and baggy shorts, his face and legs unusually brown. He stood and walked toward me and extended his hand. "Boy, we can sure use your help," he exclaimed, brushing the sweat from his forehead and into his shock of auburn hair. "We've had our hands full. I got to get home and get myself a bath and a change of clothes. I can't stand to smell myself any more." The outburst of enthusiasm surprised me. I was relieved that his personality had changed from sullen bookworm to used-car salesman.

"What am I supposed to do out here?"

"Take their money and give them a basket. Seventy-five cents if they pick them. A dollar if you do." He drove away, leaving me to sit cross-legged beneath a peach tree, observing the yellow jackets sampling the fallen fruit. Only one car passed through the gate, some Yankee man who said he'd passed some orchards a while back where he could have bought peaches for fifty cents a bushel.

"My uncle sells them for a dollar, here," I said, waiting to see if he would leave, before holding out a basket and saying, "Seventy-five cents if you pick them." He scowled and said he could get peaches cheaper somewhere else and drove off. I returned to my spot beneath the peach tree and lay down. The sun was still high when Ken returned to join me beneath the tree.

"How long are we staying out here?" I asked.

"Calder's had me out here till dark just about every night."

"Man, that's eight-thirty or nine o'clock."

"Most people won't come out here to pick until they get off work and when it isn't so hot."

Shortly after five o'clock several cars passed through the gate, and until dark a steady stream of customers took up baskets and picked from limbs burdened with fruit, paying us and leaving. By eight-thirty only a few customers remained. "Let's close it up, so nobody else comes in. When these folks leave, we're gone." It was after nine o'clock when we ate supper, and afterward, Ken invited me to go with Sara and him to the drive-in movie in Milledgeville, another unusual gesture of friendship.

The movie had already started when he parked his red-and-white Comet beside a pole, removed a speaker, and secured it in the car window beside him. He left for the concession stand and returned with three cups of Coke in a tray. "Look in the glove compartment over there, Dickey," he said, and despite Sara's protests, finished his sentence, "and give me that paper sack."

I found the sack, felt the outline of the flask inside. When Ken opened the flask I could smell the whiskey. "You ever drink any of this stuff before, Dickey?" he asked.

"A few times," I said.

"And your daddy died trying to stop it."

"God dammit, Sara, shut up," Ken said. "Drink down some of your Coke, Dickey, and I'll fix you up."

"If Imogene finds out she'll kill us all."

"I promise I won't go home and phone Imogene," Ken said. "Dickey, are you going home to tell your Mama how bad I'm corrupting you?"

"No, I promise," I simpered.

"Well, if he goes into our house like that and Mama and Daddy find out, I promise you Mama will be on the phone with Imogene tonight."

"I won't let him get drunk."

He poured the whiskey into my cup. The drink burned, but tasted fine—better than beer. Ken lit a cigarette and offered one to me. "Might as well," said I, and much to Sara's protests of "my lord" and "nobody's putting any blame on me," I lit up a Marlboro, coughed out the first puff, and decided it was best for me not to inhale. "You know," I said, chuckling at the thought. "I think this is the first time in my life I've ever been to a movie and didn't even know the name of it."

Ken laughed. "It doesn't matter. From what I can tell so far, it's one of those movies that never makes any sense anyway. Probably a two-Coke movie I'd say."

"No, Ken."

"Sara, you're getting on my nerves," Ken said, getting out of the car and heading back to the concession stand.

I took another sip of the whiskey. It tasted good. Mighty good. I felt myself begin to relax. I tossed the cigarette out the window. It was the best I'd felt since Daddy died, with the exception of that one night with Tessa Halley. Damn her hide.

Ken stopped me after two cups, but I had drunk enough to sleep that night as well as I'd slept in a long time. Until Ken, in the middle of the night, rose to respond to a knock at the bedroom door. In the darkness I heard the jingling of coins and keys as he put on his pants. "What's the matter?" I asked.

"Time to get up."

"Get up? Man, it's night time."

He opened the bedroom door and said, "Better get on up. You'll need you some breakfast before we head out."

I groaned and forced myself to stir. After putting on my pants I staggered into the kitchen and sat in a chair, propping my elbows on the table, covering my face with my hands. "Good morning, Dickey-boy," said Calder, already finished with breakfast and smoking a cigarette. "Dickey-boy's got to get up this morning ya heah. He's got to pick us some peaches."

Lanelle set a plate of waffles and link sausages before me. "Got to eat in a hurry this morning, Dickey," continued Calder. "I done messed around heah and let y'all sleep late, ya heah."

Late? I glanced at the electric clock above the freezer: 5:40 a.m. The middle of the night. "Mmph," I groaned and yawned, rubbing sleep from my eyes and staring at my plate. My head ached and my mouth was dry; the whiskey last night had affected me more than I'd thought. A second cup of coffee would help me wake up.

"Got more peaches than I know what to do with, Dickey-boy, ya heah. Can't get nothing for 'em. Cannery won't take 'em. Say they don't want 'em. They're like everybody else around here. They got more peaches than they want." He chuckled as if he were telling a joke. "Ain't had no peach crop in years, and when we do get one, we can't do nothing with 'em." He stood and reached in a pocket for his keys. Ken took his cue, gulping his last bites of waffle and following Calder out the back door. "Let's go," Ken said. I rinsed my mouth with the last of the lukewarm coffee and spat on the damp grass, getting into the Comet with Ken. We followed Calder in his pickup down the dirt road leading to the store, crossing the Macon Highway and parking on the gravel lot beside the store. Ken removed from the back of the truck two wooden signs and told me to carry one up the road toward Milledgeville. "About a hundred yards from the store. You want to give people time enough to slow down once they see it."

I walked up the highway about a football-field's length and unfolded the sign into an A.

"No, Dickey, no." I turned to see Calder waving at me. Figuring I had walked too far, I picked up the sign and walked back toward the store.

"No, on the other side."

"What?"

"Put the sign on the other side."

I turned the sign so that it faced south toward Macon.

"No," Calder hollered, waving his arms and starting up the road toward me. "The other side."

I turned the sign back around to face Milledgeville. "No, no, hell no," he yelled. "Take the damned sign to the other side of the road. The other side."

I crossed the highway and set down the sign. "Yeah, yeah," Calder hollered. "Put it down right there." Sulking, I slumped back to the parking lot where Calder had parked his truck. "Ken, you're gonna have to show Dickey what to do. Dickey-boy don't even know how to set up a sign. How are people coming from Milledgeville gonna see my sign over on this side of the road? Then Dickey wants to turn my sign toward Macon. What we gonna do with Dickey." He was trying to be funny, but I couldn't even pretend to laugh because of the lump in my throat. For a moment I wished I were back in Jefferson. Hell, it didn't matter where you were, somebody was going to ridicule you. And I had wanted to play baseball and loaf around, not get hollered at before the sun came up in the morning. "Gonna need about five bushels at the store this morning, Ken. Pick another two and leave 'em sitting ready up there." He turned and walked to the store to open it for the pulpwooders already gathered outside the door.

"Put the bigger peaches on top of these baskets. Spoiled ones put in the bucket for Calder's hogs," Ken ordered, stopping abruptly upon seeing me wrestling with a tear. I turned my face so he wouldn't see me. For a second I was afraid he might ask me what was wrong and that if I tried to answer him, I might start crying. Hell, fifteen years old, and crying. What the hell was wrong with me. "Dickey," he said. "You alright?"

I nodded.

"Calder just gets excited a lot right now. He doesn't mean anything by hollering. He's just on the verge of losing his peach crop, and he's excited. He shouldn't have hollered at you like that. But I promise you he didn't mean anything against you."

I nodded, sniffling in embarrassment. "Here," Ken said, tossing the keys onto the bed of the truck. "How about driving."

Without looking at him, I reached for the keys, grateful for his not pushing me to answer. By the time we had picked seven bushels of peaches and taken them back to the store, I had regained control, though I had little to say to Calder as we did the job of separating peaches into smaller baskets for display.

We spent most of the day at the orchard, Sara bringing sandwiches to us at noon. At mid-afternoon Calder relieved us and told us to keep store for a while. Ken and I rode down to find Ricky Lister trying to keep cool by lying shirtless on the drink cooler.

"Here, get up and let us get a drink. Get you two, Dickey. One for the road."

I removed a Coke and a Nehi Grape. "Drink the Nehi first," Ken said.

"I want the Coke," I said, bristling.

"You'll wish you had the Coke later on."

"I'm gonna drink my Coke now," I said.

"Don't get mad."

After we had returned to the orchard and Calder had left for the store, Ken said, "Let me show you something."

"What?"

"The reason you should have saved the Coke for last. I wasn't meaning to boss you, but with Ricky listening I couldn't say anything." He pried up the back seat of his car, lifted up a piece of plywood and removed two quart bottles, one filled with bourbon, the other filled with a clear liquid. He opened the large bottle containing the clear liquid and said, "Drink down some of your Grape." I gulped down about half the bottle. He filled it back up with the clear liquid, never spilling a drop.

"What is this stuff? Smells like turpentine."

"It's gin. You never had any gin?"

"I don't think so," I said, sniffing at the bottle.

"It's no good straight. You've got to mix it with something. Coke is best. I don't know about Nehi Grape. But you can try it. Who knows? You may discover a new drink. Make you famous."

I took a sip. "Not bad," I said. "Not bad at all." I turned up the drink.

"Whoa! You'd better drink that slow. It's got some wallop to it. How could I explain to Mister Calder why you're so happy out here in the peach orchard? Say, you ever play any Blackjack?"

"No."

"Five card draw?"

"No."

"That's what we'll do when we get home tonight. Play some cards. Looks like I'm gonna have to teach you a few things while you're down here. They've kept you locked up long enough."

"How about a cigarette?"

"All right. Hey, just don't get yourself hooked on them. I doubt if Imogene would appreciate your picking up all my habits while you're down here. She sent you down here a good little boy, and look at you, now. A hell-bound sinner for sure."

The days settled into a routine. Every day Ken and I rose before dawn to pick and sort and sell peaches. We spent our afternoons languishing beneath a peach tree, drinking Cokes laced with gin, blowing smoke rings or telling lewd jokes. Our job required no burden of thought and offered no rewards. We saw no need to look forward to a Saturday when Saturday could not be distinguished from Friday and Friday from Thursday; no need to refer to our watches, but to the sun, for as long as there was sunlight, there was work.

Two weeks passed before the routine was disturbed on a Sunday morning by a rain so heavy that Calder drove to the orchard about ten o'clock to send Ken and me to the house. We spent the rest of the morning beneath the overhang of the front steps until the rain slackened enough for us to begin a game of whiffleball. We hadn't played long before another downpour sent us scampering back to the porch. "Another rain delay in Atlanta," I said, imitating Milo Hamilton. "Drysdale on the mound for the Dodgers, Niekro for the Braves. Crowd of about fifty thousand disappointed, but nobody's left this stadium yet. They're still hoping to see baseball."

"Thing about baseball," Ken said, "is you sometimes have a rain-out. Football? Now that's a different story. Don't think I ever heard of a football game getting rained out."

"Only time I remember was when I was about in the second grade and Jefferson and Oglethorpe County got rained out."

"Must have been lightning."

"May have been. Though I think it had rained all day. It was like it is when you get a hurricane on the coast. One of those heavy all-day rains."

My mind drifted to thoughts of football games, of Jefferson's band breaking forth into the team's fight song, of drum cadences and cheerleaders and fans screaming, of Gus and Jim and Andrew bathing in the acclamation while I sat in the bleachers and answered questions about why I didn't play football. Truth was, I was too scared to play and everybody knew it. And when school started everyone would look down their noses at me like they had done last year, or, even worse, hardly look at me at all. "Hoard's a quitter," they would think. And some day thirty years from now would I walk into the drug store or Marlowe's Cafe where Truckie Myers and Benny Durden and Gus and Jim and others gathered daily for coffee, dressed in their coats and ties, greeting me with, "Well, if it ain't old Hoard. Y'all remember when Hoard quit the football team?" Would they always consider me a quitter? Not if I went back out for the team. And if I did that, I could appease my father and maybe even find peace with myself.

"Ken," I asked. "What's the date?"

"It's, gosh, I don't know. It's still July—I think. I'll ask Lanelle." He left and when he returned he said, "The twenty-eighth of July.

Man, this summer's about gone. Peaches won't last much longer. Don't know what this rain will do to them."

"I've been thinking."

"Uh-oh, that's dangerous, especially when you're not used to it."

"Maybe I need to go home for a few days."

"Nothing for you to do at home but go back to that radio station."

My heart sank at the thought. "No," I said. "I don't mean that. I'm talking about just for a few days, coming back maybe Wednesday or Thursday. Reckon a bus is going to Athens this afternoon?"

"You're serious, aren't you?"

"Yeah." My mind was already made up.

"Listen, Dickey, you ought to think about this some more. You're just homesick is all. Wait until tomorrow, and if you still feel like going home, then go on home."

Ricky Lister drove his mini-bike into the yard and parked it by the porch steps. "Mister Calder not gonna open up the orchard today?"

"He did open it up for a while. But nothing's going on. Nobody's out in the rain, not on a Sunday morning."

"Mister Calder ain't never closed the peach orchard on a Sunday before, even if it is raining."

"Yeah he has, Ricky. He closes it about every Sunday when he goes to church."

"Not during peach season, he don't. Not when there's this many peaches, he don't."

"Well maybe he doesn't, but he did today. If you want to go out there and sit in the peach orchard this morning, that's fine, but we're staying right here. At least I'm staying right here. Dickey's talking about going home."

"Uh-huh, Dickey's done got homesick. Wants to see his Mama."

"I ain't homesick. I just need to see a few people is all. I'll be back later in the week."

"No, you won't."

"What do you mean, 'no, you won't?'"

"I mean just what I say. You ain't coming back next week, Dickey. You ain't never coming back. Not this summer anyway."

"How do you think you know that?"

"Ricky's a psychiatrist," Ken said.

"Ain't no psychiatrist. I can just see it in Dickey's eyes. I can see it in his face."

"See what in my face?"

"You've got that far away look in your face. That homesick look."

"You're crazy."

"I may be, but I know if you go home, you ain't coming back."

The bus was halfway to Athens later that afternoon before I realized that Ricky's prophecy would prove true. Truckie Myers and Benny Durden would leave me in peace; my father would leave me in peace at my first touchdown catch and the cheers for me. I was bigger now, 145 pounds, not big by football standards but a whole hell of a lot bigger than I'd been at 120. I could do it, I told myself. Nothing—not even football practice itself—could be worse than having to spend another autumn answering the question, "Dickey, why don't you play?"

Chapter Eighteen

That evening I shocked the Methodist Youth Fellowship by showing up for a meeting for the first time since their trip to an Atlanta Hawks game back in February. Jim Smith said he "knew something was up" when I showed up at Youth Fellowship for anything other than a chili supper.

When I told him what I was thinking, his new girlfriend smiled, obviously impressed. "Dickey, you're going to play on the football team?" Her's was exactly the reaction I had hoped for. No sign from heaven could prove more inspiring. Smith offered to drive me to Coach Lofton's house that very minute. He and his girlfriend waited outside in his car as I knocked on the kitchen door of the Loftons' house. Mrs. Lofton's eyebrows raised upon seeing me. "Well, what a surprise," she said, "Sure haven't seen you around this summer." She listened with interest to my explanation until Coach Lofton came from the back room and told me to have a seat on the sofa. "Now, what can I do for you?"

"Coach, I want to come back out for football."

He laughed and said, "You're crazy, Dick. You'll get killed out there."

Maybe he was right, I thought. "But I want to play."

"We've been working out with weights all summer. We're getting bigger and stronger. And you've worked, you say, in a radio station and a peach orchard?" He laughed again and said, "I'm afraid you'll get hurt."

"I want to play."

"Well," he said, "come over to the pool tomorrow at two. That's where we've got the weights set up. But you've got some hard work ahead of you."

"I know."

"You won't get any special consideration just because you're a junior. We've got seven defensive ends right now. That means you'll be number eight. You'll have to work your way up. It'll be tough."

Ten days later on the third morning of two-a-day practices, I remembered his warnings as I sat on a bench in the locker room and gingerly tried to tie the strings on my shoulder pad, massaging my bruised right biceps with the palm of my left hand sore from a jammed finger. Beside me, teammates dressed and greeted one another grimly. "Well, there's old Hoard," Truckie Myers said upon entering. "I didn't think you'd be back today, Hoard. Figured you'd have quit again by now."

My only reply was a belch that tasted like coffee. I'd drunk two cups at breakfast and could have used another had I not been scared of puking it up on the field.

"There's no place on earth you'd rather be," cried Coach Lofton in the hallway. This man was insane, I thought. Six Flags over Georgia, Lake Lanier, my bed . . . I could think of plenty of places I'd rather be. He appeared at the door to our cage and hollered, "Jim Smith, there's no place on earth you'd rather be this morning."

Smith blinked away sleep and said, "Yes, sir," but even Smith, usually gung ho about football, failed to answer with conviction.

"Andrew, a lot of people would love to trade places with you this morning. A lot of old timers are looking back and saying, 'I'd give anything to be back out there playing football again.' You've got to love it."

Coach Lofton paused for a second and then called my name. "Dickey Hoard has come back. He missed it more than he thought, didn't you, Dickey?"

I nodded and said, "Yes, sir."

"But it's tough to come back, isn't it, Dickey? It's tough to come back."

I nodded again, because I wanted badly to quit, pack up, say to hell with it, and go home. Coach Lofton had been right all along. I was crazy. I was going to get killed. My teammates were stronger, faster, superior. He moved on down the hall to another cage.

"Sore this morning? Yeah. A lot of you are sore and wanting to drag around. This is when you begin to find out what kind of football team you're going to be. Anybody can practice the first few days when you feel good. It takes a winner to practice when he's sore and hurt. You have to look inside and see what's in your heart."

Of course I had no idea what was in my heart. I wanted to be accepted. I wanted my father proud of me. But I didn't really want to play football. Not with these guys. Benny Durden had wrestled me down one afternoon onto the floor after the locker-room toilet had overflown. Richard Smith had cracked a raw egg on my head. But there I was playing a sport I hated, hoping to silence the criticism from people I hated. Putting on my cleats I walked on the concrete floor of the hallway and stepped outside to crunch along the gravel pathway leading to the practice field. The grass on the field, recently mowed, clung to my shoes and socks. I wandered over to a line of receivers waiting to catch passes from one of the quarterbacks, until the coach of the defensive ends summoned me to follow him.

"Stevie," Coach Stoudenmire said. "Get over there at defensive end. I want you to take on the block of the fullback. Dickey, get at fullback."

I walked over to stand at a place where I figured a fullback might line up. "Now Stevie, I want you to take on the fullback with your forearm. Stay low. Hit and bounce. Don't let him get to your knee."

Get to his knee? Why, we were all wearing shorts, no knee or hip pads or any protection from the jockey strap down. I wasn't going to try to hit his knee.

"Set! Hit!" Coach Stoudenmire called. Stevie had tensed, crouching in position, preparing to hit me with his forearm when I came toward him. I stood in protest, surprising both Stevie and the coach. "Dickey," said Coach Stoudenmire. "You're the fullback. Stevie is the left defensive end. I want you blocking him like you're knocking him out of the four hole. On first hit."

Reluctantly, I crouched. "Get in a four point stance like a full-back."

I put both hands on the ground and waited on the snap count. "Set! Hit!" I ran toward Stevie, halted in front of him and bumped his shoulder pad as Stevie struck my ribs with his forearm.

"Coach Lofton, send me Truckie Myers down here." Truckie jogged over to our group. "Truckie, get over there at fullback and block the end for me. Watch him, Dickey, so you can see what I want out of you."

On the count, Truckie ran full speed toward Stevie's legs, and Stevie smashed him with a forearm, giving ground for only a fraction of a second before bouncing off the block. "Good job, Stevie. Now, Dickey, that's what I want out of you. One more time, Stevie, with Dickey blocking."

He called the signal. I ran and lunged at Stevie's feet. He pushed my head into the ground, wet grass clinging to my facemask and hands as I stood. "Keep your feet on the block, Dickey. Don't duck your head. You'll get killed if you duck your head."

Twice more the coach made me block Stevie, then told me to line up at defensive end, and although the whistle blew to end pre-practice, he made me fight off the blocker anyway and the collision jarred me. I shook my head as the team gathered for side-straddle hops and stretching exercises and neck bridges and the dreaded grass drills, where we ran in position until the whistle sounded for us to fall on our chests, quickly bouncing to our feet to run in place again, falling at the whistle. After grass drills came offensive fundamental period, when we tried to block an opposing player holding a padded dummy while straddling a two-by-twelve plank. When my turn came, I lunged at Stevie, but failed to budge him, stumbled and picked up a splinter in my hand. I hollered.

"What happened? He step on your hand?"

"No, I got a splinter."

"Well, you better get used to that, son, if you can't block any better than that. You'll pick up lots of splinters on the bench. Try it again."

I failed to budge Red Simpson holding the dummy. "You've got to keep those big size twelves moving, son," hollered the line coach.

Later efforts brought more scoldings. "You can't just titty-bump with the man, son, and think you're gonna move him. You've got to explode into him." He shoved a dummy into my hands and illustrated by attacking it, catching me off guard and knocking me to the ground. The linemen laughed. Even the coach couldn't suppress his grin as he shook his head. Moving from the boards to begin another drill, he called, "Give me three men on offense, three men with dummies on defense. Base blocking."

I walked forward to the line of scrimmage, positioning myself as a blocker. "I said, 'three men,'" yelled the coach. "You grab one of those dummies, son, and try not to get hurt."

Every practice brought pain and humiliation. Every waking minute was consumed or haunted by football; morning practice, weight lifting, team meeting, specialty sessions for receivers and quarterbacks and kickers, afternoon practice, supper, collapse, morning practice, and so on until finally, after a Saturday morning scrimmage, we were given a day and a half to recover. Mostly I slept or watched television with the fan blowing at full speed on me. I was too drained from a week of heat and exertion to even want to leave the house.

Monday morning the alarm clock rang at seven o'clock, but I couldn't rouse myself from bed. Mammie responded to my groans by poking a thermometer beneath my tongue, returning minutes later to remove it and say, "Yes, it's over a hundred. A hundred and one. You'll have to stay in the bed today, Doll-boy." She tucked the sheet around me, drawing it up beneath my chin.

"Call Coach Lofton and tell him I can't come to practice," I groaned. "But be sure to tell him I'm sick." For two days I stayed in the house, relieved that I was sick enough to avoid practice, but anxious because I knew I would not rise from the role of scrub and holder of a dummy by lying in bed. Wednesday morning I awoke still feeling weak, but without any fever. I decided to try to practice.

"Thought for sure you'd quit, Hoard," Truckie said when I walked in. "I told everybody, 'yeah, old Hoard decided it was too tough for him.' What did you do? Decide to just take a few days off?"

"I've been sick."

"Him been sick. Well bless his heart. Did him hurt and have a temperature?"

Looking around the room, I saw that his taunts had gained the attention of several others. I said nothing except, "Yeah, I had a fever."

The morning's practice was held at the stadium. After a few minutes of exerting myself in the humid air, I already felt weak, and as the morning grew hotter, my legs began to feel shaky. I malingered on the sideline as often as possible during drills and when the scrimmage started, I rested on one knee, hoping for mercy from Coach Lofton because of my sickness. But he showed none, as if he'd forgot all about it, continuing to call me back out to scrimmage. It was hot. My body ached for water. I sank to one knee between plays. I had no energy.

"Let's have a little life," Coach Lofton hollered. "We are dragging around this morning. If you don't like this, you don't like the game. All we're doing here this morning is playing football." His exhortations inspired only a few cries of "A little life, a little life, now," echoed without conviction and quickly dying. Words consumed energy best left in reserve for the heat. The sun burned high in a cloudless sky. No breeze. Steamy. Again an exhortation. Again half-hearted cries of "Come on now, let's have some life." But the only genuine fervor erupted when Coach Lofton finally blew his whistle to proclaim, "Let's bring it up," and the team gathered around him, removing helmets and soaked jerseys, sweat dripping from foreheads, t-shirts drenched and already soured. Boys were eager to jump in the swimming pool, go home for lunch, mark off from the calendar another morning practice.

"Wait a minute," Coach Stoudenmire said, his words carrying a hint of threat. His lips contorted into a half smile. "We've dragged around here all morning. We've got a football game two weeks from Friday, and we didn't do a whole lot this morning toward getting ready for it. We can't afford to have any more practices like this one. Now you're going to have to make up your minds that when you come to practice, you're going to work, and that either you work during practice or you'll work afterwards. Now, I think you all agree today that we're going to have to work afterwards. You can leave off your shoulder pads, but put your helmets back on. Seniors, form a line across the forty and lead us in calisthenics."

Grimly the eight seniors lined up, underclassmen forming lines facing them. "Alright, Jack," Coach Stoudenmire said. "Side-straddle hops. Ten repetitions."

Jack Kesler nodded and encouraged us to do them right. "Side-straddle hop," he called. "Ten repetitions. Ready?"

"Ready."

"Exercise."

"One, two, three, ONE, one, two, three, TWO, one, two, three, THREE. . . ."

After the tenth count coach Stoudenmire hollered for us to do ten grass drills "On the whistle." He sounded it. "Let's pick 'em up. Knees high, running in place." When he was finally satisfied that everyone was running with knees high enough, he blew the whistle and we hit the ground.

"UP!" he hollered.

"ONE."

"Alright, get 'em up. High, high, get 'em up. And I want you to bounce up quick off the ground. Don't lie there and crawl up. Hit and bounce up." The whistle blew and we hit the ground.

"UP!"

"TWO."

The whistle blew and we hit the ground. "UP!"

"THREE!"

After the twelfth one, two extra (one for my not getting back to my feet quick enough, which drew some angry reproofs from the seniors), Coach Stoudenmire commanded Truckie to lead us in another set of side-straddle hops. "Side-straddle hops. Ten repetitions. Ready?"

"Ready."

"Exercise."

Each of the eight seniors led us in ten repetitions of a calisthenic, followed by a set of ten grass drills. "Come on, Dickey, pick it up," someone hollered. I gasped for breath, until halfway through the final set I collapsed, exhausted, unable to stir. "Come on, Dickey," yelled the line coach. "Get up. Get to your feet, son."

But I couldn't budge. I could only suppose that those around me continued to respond to the whistle. I lay still. "Come on, son," the line coach said, his voice above me. "It's over." A few seconds passed before I pulled myself to my knees, swaying as I managed to stand, nearly falling again as I stooped to pick up my shoulder pads. I had ceased sweating and my mouth felt like it was stuffed with cotton. Saying nothing, I staggered across the field and pulled myself slowly up the grandstand steps. "Get out of the way, Hoard," said Benny Durden shoving past me up the steps.

"Slowing down traffic, Dickey."

"He slowed us down all day," Benny said. "He's the big reason we were out there so long."

At the top of the steps I pressed along the concrete walkway through the gates of the swimming pool, stripped to my jockey strap and fell into the water, sinking to the bottom of the diving area, pushing myself with my toes back toward the surface, grabbing the deck to pull my face and shoulders from the pool.

"You alright, Hoard?" The voice was Smith's. "You look like a ghost."

"I don't feel so good." I groaned.

"What?"

"I'm still sick."

He left me alone for a few minutes to lie with my head on the hot concrete, my body in the cold water, before returning to tell me, "I've got to pick up my mother at work. You still want me to take you home?"

"Yeah."

Retrieving my equipment, I followed Smith to his car, walking past Coach Lofton, who stood grinning at someone near the front gate. "Coach, I said. "I think I'm still sick."

He felt my forehead and his grin faded. "Yeah, Dick, I'd say you're right. I don't know what you've got, probably some kind of bug, but you'd better go get yourself back in the bed until you get over this thing. Drink you plenty of fluids."

When I got home Mammie took my temperature. My fever was 103. For two more days I stayed in bed and didn't return to practice until Monday. I thought about quitting, but it would have been doing the same thing I'd done more than two years earlier when Daddy was alive; I couldn't fail him again. Anyway, I couldn't have stood the label of quitter. I may have hated football, but some things were worse.

Chapter
Nineteen

After spending the rest of the week in bed, I returned to practice and had what I thought was a decent week, making a few tackles in scrimmage. After scouting our opponents on Friday night, I was inspired for our final scrimmage in full uniform on Saturday morning, assisting on some stops, even after the line coach had moved me to defensive tackle. "Read the tackle's head just like you'd read the end's," he said. "Four-point stance." The offensive tackle's head went straight up and back. Pass block. "Pass, pass," I hollered, dodging the blocker and rushing the quarterback, Woody Herbert. When I'd nearly reached him, Stevie Underwood, the defensive end, grabbed him and slung him toward the ground. Woody's left leg swung around like a whip over the top of my facemask. His foot hit my nose. Stunned, I sank to my knees and shook my head.

"Don't be so rough on my quarterback," Coach Lofton shouted. "Stop at the point of contact on the quarterback."

Groggy, I found the huddle, my hand on my face. "You okay, Dickey?" Randall Brewer, the middle guard asked. "You need out?"

"No, I'm alright. I just got hit on my nose."

He grabbed my face mask and pulled it down to get a clear view. "Gaw, you sure did. You sure you don't want out?"

"Nah, I'll be alright," I said, wanting to finish the scrimmage, and earn myself some playing time for next week's game.

When the scrimmage ended we walked up the grandstand steps to the parking lot and I claimed a seat near the back of the bus. Removing my helmet I gingerly felt my nose. It seemed swollen. "Gus," I said as he sat down in front of me. "Does my nose look swollen to you?"

His eyes grew wide. "Hoard," he laughed. "Your nose is whompsided."

"Nah!"

"I mean it. It's whompsided. Come here, Goose, and look at Hoard's nose and see if it ain't whompsided."

"Hot'll mighty, Hoard. It sure is. Look, Benny, at how whompsided Hoard's nose is."

Benny looked at me and said, "Looks like somebody straightened it out to me."

I grinned. This was one of their jokes. "Look in the mirror, Hoard, if you don't believe me," Gus said.

"I'll look in the mirror," I said, walking to the driver's seat, "but I don't believe you." I looked in the rearview mirror and saw that my nose had been kicked over beneath my left eye. "Your nose is broke, boy," cried Goose.

He was right. My afternoon was spent in Doctor Griffith's office. An instrument that looked like thongs was poked up my nostrils, and then the doctor popped my nose back into position before packing it with gauze and covering it with tape and telling me I could practice again on Thursday, but only if I attached a full facemask, called a bird cage, to my helmet.

On Friday night I peered through the bars of the bird cage as the final seconds of our opening game ticked away. Jefferson thirty-nine; Oconee County thirteen. The freshmen had played much of the fourth quarter. Everyone in uniform had played, except me. One minute left, and our offense fumbled. "Give me a defense out there," Coach Lofton shouted. Bill Elder and Andrew ran out again to play defensive ends with the game still safely out of reach.

During the entire fourth quarter I had stood close to Coach Stoudenmire, hoping he'd put me in the game. But with a minute left, I moved behind him, out of his view, crowded amid the starters now walking without their helmets, their wet hair mussed from the sweat of battle; I was still wearing my helmet, rehearsing my excuse for being the only one among the twenty-five dressed out who didn't play. "Broken nose, still not well. I hope by next week, I'll be ready."

"Has anybody not played?" Coach Lofton hollered. Forty seconds. I limped behind the team. It would help to limp. All those people whose eyes bored into the back of my head asking the same question, "has anybody not played?" and seeing me limp, could find reason for their answer. "Yes. One player has not played. Number forty-two. Who is that? He's not in the program" (and I wasn't, thank God, having come out for the team two days after picture day). But someone would know and would proclaim, "It's Dickey. Dickey Hoard has not played." "But look, is he limping? Is Dickey Hoard limping?" "Yes, he's limping. Sprained ankle, maybe?" "Yeah, and didn't he break his nose?" "Yes, he did." "That's why Dickey is the only one who hasn't played. A sprained ankle and a broken nose."

Thirty seconds. Twenty.

"Dickey Hoard." Coach Lofton's voice seemed to rise above the thousands and above the honks and toots and drum beats of the band playing "Proud Mary."

"Oh, God, no," I thought. "Don't let him put me in there. Not now."

"Dickey Hoard, get in there at defensive end." Fifteen seconds left and I ran sweatless onto the field, white pants shining next to the brown and green stains of my teammates. Ten seconds. Five. Oconee County to the line. One play. Pass. Rush the quarterback. He threw long downfield. The horn sounded. The pass fell incomplete. The game ended. Fans spilled onto the field. Teammates congratulated one another, taking off their helmets. I kept mine on, head down, avoiding looking at anyone as I walked alone to the bus. Nothing could be more humiliating.

Or so I thought. The lowest moment came two week's later when I was made to play in a B-team game with sophomores and freshmen. I needed some game experience, Coach Lofton had told Coach Knight, instructing him to leave me in the game for every down.

Midway through the third quarter, after three straight long pass routes, I could barely raise my arms. Exhausted, gasping for breath, I prayed to be taken out for maybe two or three plays, but Coach Knight kept me in the game. I struggled before the varsity players and coaches observing from the grandstand. "You were sucking wind out there, Hoard," was Smith's accurate evaluation. Ineligible to dress out for a second game in one week, I sold programs the next night with the other B-team players outside the stadium gates. Whenever possible I evaded people I knew, though I'd been unable to dodge Woody Herbert's mother, who cornered me for a program and asked, "Are you hurt again, Dickey?"

"No, ma'am."

"Well, what are you doing out here? Why aren't you with the team?"

"I—uh—I played in the B-team game yesterday, so I can't dress out."

"B-team? I didn't know a junior could play B-team."

Ducking my head, I tried to think of a quick lie. The B-team was short of ends and would have had to forfeit if I hadn't helped them? No, her son would only tell her the truth. What was the use of lying? Red-faced, I grinned and gave Mrs. Herbert her change and said, "I guess they can. I'm a junior, alright, and they made me play."

The six more weeks of football looming over me may as well have been six more years. I was a disgrace, a junior playing behind freshmen. The worst player on the team. The best thing that could happen to me would be to die. I might go to hell, but at least I'd be out of Jefferson. Dying, now that would shake up the school, I thought. Probably make all the papers. "Dickey Hoard, son of slain Piedmont Solicitor Floyd Hoard, was found dead apparently of self-inflicted wounds. . . ." Yeah, that would shake up the school; they'd all be sorry then. Kill myself the day before the Commerce game. Maybe the team would all wear black patches on their sleeves. Have a moment of silence to remember me before the game. Maybe even have a memorial service instead of the pep rally on Friday. Bring my body into the auditorium and open the casket. Let 'em all file by. Yeah, they'd be sorry, then. Imagine all those girls like Tessa and Marie feeling guilty and saying, "I'll never forgive myself," and "why didn't I let him know I loved him while he was alive." Had they tried, they could have loved me, but maybe it took someone's dying before anybody could ever realize it. Like my father. I hadn't known how much I'd loved him until he was dead.

My mother kept a pistol in the drawer beside her bed. The next afternoon, I removed it from its holster. All six chambers were loaded. Mammie was in the kitchen, my little sisters in the living room. I picked up the gun, and with my hand trembling, carried it to my room. In my mouth? Or right between my eyes? Wasn't that how people did it? Or maybe right in the temple. That should do it, I thought. I put the gun to my head. Do it. By tonight, the whole town would know. The whole town will be shaken. It'll be in all the newspapers. Gainesville. Athens. Atlanta. Do it. I placed my finger on the trigger. My heart had already stopped beating. One squeeze and it was all over. Or was it? If there was a hell for murderers, would I go there for killing myself? Would I burn for the grief I'd bring on Mammie? Right beside Cliff Park who would burn for the grief he'd brought on me?

Looking back I shudder at how close I'd come to ending it—over football? No, it was deeper than football, though I couldn't put it into words. The unfairness of life. The selfishness I saw around me. My father's death was like someone had hammered a nail into my senses and the infection was spreading. I hated the whole world, hated myself, could not see any sense of worth unless someone were pinning a varsity letter on me or applauding me for some game-winning shot. I didn't need to be a star football player. I just needed to be seen as important to the team. One more week, I told myself at the time. Give life one more week. Lowering the pistol I carried it back to Mama's room.

Chapter
Twenty

There was a ray of hope the next Friday night. In the final minutes of a fairly close game with Commerce I got to play the last seven plays; maybe I'd done better in the B-team game than I thought. And maybe, I hoped, I had performed well enough for those seven plays against Commerce to earn another chance, perhaps at least find myself on one of the specialty teams, kickoff or punt team, or one of the return teams, just to have the chance to run on the field for a few plays against Morgan County so that the spectators would know I was needed for something.

But Thursday, as the team sat in the physical-education classroom before practice and Coach Lofton listed on the chalk board the offensive team, the defensive team, the kickoff team, the punt team, the kickoff receiving team, the punt receiving team, my name was again absent from all of them.

Despondent, I held a dummy during practice as the first-team offense ran through plays. "Come on, Dickey. I know we're not in pads but let's make it look like something over there." I wanted to throw down the dummy and walk off, tell Coach Lofton I'd had enough and that the whole team could go to hell and find someone else to hold their dummies. By God I was leaving. This very night I was leaving this little hellhole town that had killed my father and would kill me as well. Tonight, by God. Where I was going I had no idea, but I was going somewhere.

"See you, Gus," I said after he'd driven me to my house. "Hope y'all whip them tomorrow."

"What kind of talk is that, Hoard? Y'all whip them? You're part of this team, too."

"I won't be playing," I said and slammed his car door and went straight to my bedroom. I tore a sheet of paper from my notebook and scribbled a brief note letting the family know they were not to blame. "It's nothing I can explain," I wrote. "It's just something I've got to do. One day in a few years, when I get things sorted out, I'll be back to visit. Don't worry about me. I'll be fine." I set the note beneath some socks in my top drawer. They would probably go hunting for a note; if not, one day when they cleaned out my stuff to give away, they would find the note and know I'd not been kidnaped and murdered.

Removing a few pairs of socks, I threw them into my duffel bag, the same one I used during basketball season. Maybe during basketball season, people would remember me. "Dickey may have been the worst football player in Jefferson, but he was a good basketball player. Can't even come to a basketball game without thinking about him." I tossed some underwear and shirts into the bag and removed from a white sock the fifty dollars Calder had paid me for working those two weeks in his orchard, and lay down on the bed, a lump rising in my throat at the magnitude of what I was doing. Well, at least I wasn't killing myself. This was not as bad as suicide. A fellow wouldn't go to hell for running away.

Mammie called me for supper. Hardly tasting my food, I cleaned my plate and drank several glasses of tea, blankly staring at nothing. After brushing my teeth, I put my toothbrush and a new tube of toothpaste into the duffel bag, then lay again on my bed and stared at the top bunk above me, my literature book open beside me in case someone entered. My head pounded. Pent-up sobs seemed lodged in my throat. I lay there until after eight o'clock before sneaking down the hall for a final look at my little sisters, who lay on the floor watching television. They would be grown women the next time they saw me. And Mammie? It was my last look at Mammie. I suppressed a sob, and returned to the room and picked up the duffel bag and carried it out the back door and around the fence beside the funeral home, then up the street beside Albert's. My plan was to walk to the interstate and catch a ride to South Carolina, find a job and make enough money to live on. Come back some day bringing with me the beautiful woman I'd married and our baby to meet the family, driving a Cadillac, letting my friends admire it and ask me how I'd done so well to buy it, and I'd tell them all my story: all it had taken was for me to gain the chance to start over, to get away from all the influences of Jefferson and the people wanting me to be something I was not.

The wind blew dry leaves along the sidewalk near the Baptist church, leaves falling from trees surrounding the parking lot. I buttoned the top button of my overcoat and turned toward the high school and my final look at the place where people seemed to have suffocated me with their indifference. What would my classmates say tomorrow? Con Underwood might tell others that they should all have seen it coming; he confessed that he thought my mind had snapped one day last year during Mrs. Smith's lesson on "perception and point of view." Prior to class she had secretly instructed me to listen for a verbal cue, leap from my desk, snatch her purse, and run from the room. I had sat tensely that morning, heart racing, listening for the cue, and upon hearing her say, "few people see an event in the same way," leaped up to grab the purse, expecting to hear an explosion of laughter as I ran from the room. But no one had laughed. I had made it all the way down the hall to the boys' restroom before the astonished class suddenly gasped out it's nervous response. While waiting until Mrs. Smith had sent someone to get me, I quaked inside without understanding why. "How come nobody laughed or said anything?" I had asked Con after class.

"I don't know," he had said. "Maybe everybody was feeling like I was. Sort of a sinking feeling, like, 'Well, it finally happened. Dickey snapped. And there he goes.'"

Yeah, Con would probably say he had seen it coming. But most of them would be stunned.

A car suddenly pulled from a side road, headlights aimed at me. I bolted, started to run, but decided that, no, running would only call attention to me, and anyway, the driver had probably already spotted me. And so I walked ahead, nonchalantly, as if headed toward a friend's house, though I knew that once the news got out that I'd run away someone would be proudly saying that they were sure they were the last to have seen Dickey Hoard in Jefferson, leaving town about 8:30 on that Thursday, heading north to the interstate. But where would they think I was headed? Atlanta, of course. They would never suspect I'd hitched a ride north toward Greenville.

The car passed. I couldn't believe what I saw. My mother's station wagon. But she was supposed to be at bridge club until ten. Did she recognize me? She had to. The lights had shone right in my face. The car turned in the parking lot behind me. Should I run? No, what good would it do? I walked straight ahead, the lights coming up from behind me. "Dickey?" my mother said.

I halted.

"Where are you going?"

"Nowhere."

"Well, get in the car and I'll take you wherever it is you're going."

Silently, defeated, I entered the car, my heart pounding, my throat swollen.

"I was sitting there at bridge club and had the strangest feeling that I had to leave—that something was wrong. I had no idea what. I just had a feeling I couldn't shake, like something was telling me, 'you need to go home.' I guess everything is alright back at the house." She waited for a reply that wasn't coming. "Where are you going?"

I shook my head and gritted my teeth in an effort to suppress a sob.

"I don't mind if you want to go some place. Maybe you feel like you want to go talk to somebody. I don't mind you going off, but please just always tell mother or someone where you're going. Now, where were you going?"

"Nowhere?" I said, my voice breaking.

"Dickey, you were going somewhere. You weren't just taking a walk, not with your duffel bag. Were you wanting to go off somewhere to spend the night? Were you going to Bill Elder's?"

I said nothing.

"Where were you going?"

"Away," I sobbed. "Just—away."

"But why?"

"I can't—can't—stand it—stand it—here—any—any more."

Chapter
Twenty-one

Shadows lengthened across the remnants of earless and tawny corn-stalks leaning in fields, across cows with thoughtless gazes chewing their cud in pastureland. The bus was grinding toward Morgan County, its occupants keeping the sanctity expected of those approaching battle, though a few seniors risked setting a poor example by distracting themselves with lesser gods. "You going deer hunting in the morning, Goose?"

"You betcha. We're heading out as soon as we get back tonight."

"Got you a deer stand?"

"Yep. My uncle's got us one in Green County."

A year had passed since my ride with Tessa. Within two weeks of that ride she was going steady with a football player who had his own car and money for enough flowers to probably coax her out of her panties. Ignorant bitch, Tessa Halley, just like all of them, like the girl sitting behind me today in class bragging to a friend, "I'm going to the Homecoming Dance with this boy from Winder, and guess what? He has a red sports car. Do you believe it? Can't you just see me driving up to the Homecoming Dance in a red sports car?," leaving me shaking my head and cursing her. Did the boy have a name? Would she go with him if he drove a pickup truck? Why the hell didn't she spare him the agony of spending an evening with her in hopes of her "putting out"? Why not rent her own sports car and go to the dance with the person she loved the most—herself? What she needed was someone to tell her what a stupid and heartless bitch she was and what she really deserved—to rot in hell, and help her to see it by putting a knife to her throat and dangling her over the fires so that maybe she would wake up and see how stupid she was to lose her virginity to a sports car. And if she did put out in exchange for a ride in a sports car, she was nothing but a whore. God in heaven, help, was that how all girls' minds worked? If so, there wasn't a girl in the school who didn't need someone to put the fear of hell in their lives. Maybe I had to do it. Maybe I could run away again, and this time, while everyone searched for me in South Carolina, hide out in one of those vacant upstairs rooms at the church, come out at night and start killing off one by one all the girls in my class. But not just my class. All the classes. Maria Jensen. Truckie's girlfriend. Kill them all. Slash Marie Nunnally's throat. Let her whimper and cry and plead with me for her life. Let the GBI gradually discover the clues. "These girls' throats have all been slashed since the day Dickey Hoard disappeared. I theorize that he's still in town and he is the one killing them."

Ha! How would Tessa feel then? Would she feel the terror, wondering when she would be next? Would she lie awake at night fearful at the thought of me?

"Hey, Hoard," Smith said, interrupting my thoughts. "What are you so quiet for?"

"Y'all be quiet now," Benny Durden said. "Dickey's getting himself all fired up for the game."

"Why? He ain't gonna play."

Several boys snickered. I clenched my teeth and my fists, but kept my vigil of silence, having said nothing to them all day. Just because I had to live among them didn't mean I had to talk to them. And anyway, they would pay for their taunts. This whole town would pay, grieving over their teenaged dead.

"How about you, Truckie? You going deer hunting?"

"No, he's dear hunting. The two legged kind."

"Well does he plan on skinning and eating her?," came the question followed by an explosion of laughter, which drew the ire of

Coach Lofton, who told them they'd better get their minds on playing a football game.

I kept silent until halftime in the locker room. The score was tied at six. While the coaches had drawn play adjustments on a chalkboard and bandaged cuts as the players sat on benches or on the concrete floor I sipped at a soft drink and watched indifferently as Coach Stoudenmire pressed his hands along Stevie Underwood's side, "Does it hurt here?"

"Uh-uh, no sir."

"How about here?"

Stevie grimaced in reply.

"Probably a hip pointer," said Coach Stoudenmire. "It's painful, but we're going to have to keep you in there. We'll rest you if you can't go."

"I can go," declared Stevie.

"Everybody's alright, but Stevie," Coach Stoudenmire said shortly before the team returned to the field. "We probably ought to let somebody else go down for him on the kickoff team."

"Alright," Coach Lofton shouted. "We need someone for Stevie on the kickoff team." Glancing up, I saw that he was looking down at me. "Dickey Hoard. You can go down on the kickoff team."

I nodded and finally broke my vigil. "Yes, sir," I said.

We kicked off to start the second half. I trotted onto the field and lined up in position, tensing for the whistle, ready to throw myself full speed into an advancing body. I ran forward as Simpson shanked the kick to his right, the ball bouncing a few times before a Morgan County player picked it up and stumbled to the turf. The whistle ended the play before a man had ever blocked me. "Damn, Simpson," I muttered as I jogged off the field. Next time at least give me a chance to get knocked on my butt.

But there was no next time; the offense failed to score in the second half, fumbled late in the game at our own twenty-two yard line, and gave up the winning touchdown eight plays later. The horn sounded and we trudged to the locker room, some boys shedding tears of frustration as I cursed them under my breath for losing. They were too worried about hunting deer or luring their slutty girlfriends into the back of a car to win football games. And to think people had predicted they'd win the state championship, to think that I'd actually held them in awe because I thought they were so damned much better, faster, stronger than me. Not any more. Morgan County sure as hell hadn't been afraid of them, so why should I? They collapsed on benches in the locker room, crying like babies, while I looked on in disgust, knowing I would never let them intimidate me again.

After an hour-and-a-half Monday of two long periods of fundamental drills, the whistle blew to end the five-minute break. "Alright, give me the offense over here," Coach Lofton shouted. I threw down half a cup of ice and kicked it from my path. The first string offense had responded to the call by offering some unconvincing calls to enthusiasm while jogging to huddle beneath the goal posts at the stadium. Coach Lofton decided to practice here because he hoped the move from the drab practice field behind the school to the inspiring scenery of a stadium beneath the lights would lift the vision of a team that had played five games and won only two.

"I've got it," I told Bill Elder, pushing him away from the defensive end's position. He opened his mouth as if to protest, but I glared him into submission. "I've got it." I said.

"Alright," he said. "I'll get you in four plays."

I gave no reply. I might not be able to run away from home without getting caught or have the nerve to pull the trigger on myself, but I could throw myself headlong into charging bodies in the hope of dying or at least getting hurt badly enough that I never had to play football again. Like a crazed soldier charging up a treeless hill toward the machine guns, I would take their best shots until they dragged me off.

Coach Lofton called a play. The offense broke huddle with a careless clap of hands, walked to the line and settled into their stances. Simpson lined up at tight end across from me. "Set! Hit!," bellowed Herbert, taking the snap and handing the ball to Jack Kesler behind the right guard. I dodged past Simpson, fired all the way down the line and knocked Jack down as he tried to dance away from the middle guard. To my surprise, I felt no pain. The collision had not been violent enough, I supposed. I'd have to throw myself into him even harder next time.

Stunned, Jack looked at me and said, "Good hit, Dickey."

"Come on. Let's run it again," Coach Lofton hollered. "Nothing but base blocking. Somebody got whipped. On the line. Let's run it."

They repeated the play and I tackled Jack again behind the line. "Come on, that should have been there. We had the linebacker blocked. Who made the tackle?"

"The defensive end."

"Oh, come on! What's the defensive end doing way down there? Dickey, you knew it was coming. Don't cheat on us."

"Cheat," I thought sardonically. "Is that what Morgan County did? Cheat? They didn't stand around and let themselves get blocked. Neither will I. Run something else, and I'll stop it just like they did."

The next play Coach Lofton directed toward me. Simpson blocked down on the tackle and the fullback lumbered toward me. I side-stepped him and met the halfback head on. "Whoo! Good lick, Dickey Hoard. Good lick."

They tried next to run around my end. I fought past a blocker, stepped behind him to penetrate into the backfield and wrapped my left arm around the back and pulled him to the ground. The next call went around the far end. I scrambled down the line, and when Smith cut back toward an empty gap, I blind-sided him. He threw the ball down in frustration three yards behind the line of scrimmage and snarled, "Play your position, Hoard."

"Can't get out of the backfield," I sneered. "Can't even get past me, much less Morgan County."

Come on, I thought. Come at me, you sons of bitches. I forgot about getting killed. These guys couldn't kill me. Hell, I was killing them. On the next play, Gus, who outweighed me by forty pounds, lumbered toward me with the ball. He'd flatten me for sure if I stood straight up, I figured, so I put a shoulder beneath his knee. He went forward, but down. I could do it. I could tackle every back on this team. Why, they couldn't even whip their own lousy scrubs. No wonder Morgan County had shut them down.

"Can't somebody stop Dickey Hoard?" Coach Lofton cried.

"Hell, no," I muttered. Nobody on the offensive line said a word. They couldn't stop me. They couldn't stop anybody. And that was their whole damned problem.

When the practice ended I sauntered off the field, my fists clenched, expecting threats and derision from the seniors. Let them provoke me. I had my helmet off now, holding it by the bird cage, and would swing it like a hammer against them. I'd fight any one of them on the spot, and be back tomorrow to humiliate them again at practice. I glared at Truckie and Benny, waiting for them to say something. "Whatever you ate before you came to practice, Hoard," Benny Durden said, "I hope you eat it again tomorrow."

Bill Elder grabbed my shoulder from behind. "Good practice, Hoard," he said. "You keep that up, buddy, and you'll be starting this Friday night."

I sneered in reply.

"You made it tough on us today," Gus said to me as he drove me home. "We need it to be tough. You have another practice like that tomorrow, here?"

No doubt I had snapped, had gone absolutely crazy. I just happened to have done so on the football field, so that rather than wearing a straight jacket I was wearing shoulder pads, so that rather than getting wrestled down and a tranquilizer shot into my hip, I was congratulated.

The next two days I worked out with the first team defense. When we met in the physical-education classroom on Thursday for our team meeting I was singled out for helping turn around our team's attitude. I watched my name go up on the board for the kickoff team, the punt team, and for a "series," which meant that on alternating possessions I would play right defensive end. The next night after we beat Putnam County 39–14 in the rain, I walked off the field wearing a dirty uniform and a smile.

I figured I had played pretty well. But during the Sunday afternoon film session my confidence was shaken when I learned that my grade was less than fifty percent. When Coach Stoudenmire called out my grade, I heard a few muttered sneers, but felt encouraged when he explained, "Don't let the poor grade fool you. Most of the minuses came when the play went away from Dickey and he didn't stay at home. He wants to be in on every tackle, but when the play goes away from him, he can't go chasing the ball carrier. Now Dickey, we suspect Hephzibah will try to hurt us with some screens and reverses after scouting us, but we'll have you ready. Your mistakes were aggressive mistakes and we can live with aggressive mistakes."

Relieved that my poor grade didn't mean a banishment to the bench, I worked at practice, Coach Stoudenmire watching my every move. "Alright, we're not expecting you to make the tackle on that play. All we want you to do is clog up the hole . . . remember to check for screens and reverses . . . if the end releases for a pass, hold him up, break up the timing of the play, then outside rush and keep containment . . . don't get to thinking so much that you forget to give us a good initial lick."

By Wednesday's practice I had grown more confident, having been exposed in three days to practically every situation a defensive end could face—sweeps, screen passes, roll-out passes—no longer having to hesitate before reacting. "A good practice, a good practice," Coach Lofton shouted at the end of the session. "We look like we're getting ready for a football game Friday night."

The team roared its readiness, enthusiasm high after Friday's victory. I roared with the rest of them because I now felt a part of the team, had helped win the game as much as anybody, could look them in the eye without shame for I'd be on the field with them again Friday night. "Tomorrow afternoon, our team meeting right after school, then practice in sweats and helmets. Let's get ready for Hephzibah."

After we showered and dressed at the school, Gus offered me a ride home. "Good practice, Hoard," he said as he pulled in to the driveway.

"Thanks."

"You've come a long way the past two weeks. I used to could block you easy. You're getting to be the hardest man on the team for me to block. I'm glad to see it. You're helping this team. You hear me?"

"Yeah."

"Only thing is, you've done gone and got too serious on me. What's going on with you? I used to could count on you for a good laugh. When this season is over, some night after a basketball game and you've scored about twenty-five points, me and you'll go out and celebrate. You remember that night, Hoard?"

I chortled and said, "Yeah."

"A couple of beers would do you good," he said. "Don't get me wrong. I'm not touching it until the season is over. But when it's over, we'll have us a good time. Well, see you tomorrow."

But I didn't see Gus nor any of my teammates the next day; the telephone rang the next morning before Mama had left for work. Daddy's mother had died in Griffin. A stroke and then a fatal heart attack. Yes, Mama said, she would try to make it there this afternoon. Would any of the girls ride with her, she asked? No. They would stay in school. Would I ride? Not if I had to risk losing any playing time at football. Only after phoning Coach Stoudenmire to see if my missing school and practice would alter my status, and only after he'd assured me my position was safe, I consented to ride with Mama to my father's home town, where for the first time since Daddy's funeral I saw members of his family.

Mama and I sat at my Aunt Eunice's kitchen table and drank coffee as Eunice relived her mother's last hours: "Imogene, Mother was lying in the bed and she called me in there and told me, 'Eunice, Fuzzy's been here,' and I said, 'you saw Fuzzy here?,' and she said, 'yeah, it was Fuzzy. He was right there at the foot of the bed and he was dressed in white and smiling at me. Eunice,' she said, 'I believe he wants me to go with him.' And you know it wasn't an hour later that she was gone."

A chill climbed my back at my grandmother's delirium. She must have lost her mind there at the end. I stared at my coffee cup lest

Eunice see the incredulity in my face, or was it embarrassment I felt at hearing mentioned so matter-of-factly something of the afterlife. When the oxygen was cut off from the brain people suffered hallucinations. It was the principle behind intoxication, a lack of oxygen to the brain. "Imogene," she said. "I'm inclined to believe she really saw him."

I stole a glance at my aunt. She seemed in earnest. Had she lost her mind? Maybe the shock of her mother's death was pushing her to the edge of sanity. It was one thing to lie near death and suffer delirium, another thing for the living to believe such hallucinations true. "Yes," she said. "I think she really saw him."

Another spasm climbed my back as the kitchen door opened and for a brief instant I believed in my grandmother's final vision; for there he stood, thick hair combed back, a smile crossing his face as he loosened the tie beneath the dark coat, exhaling smoke from a lit cigarette. My mouth hanging open, tears welling in my eyes, a lump thickening in my throat, I could say nothing, merely stare at him until he broke the silence. "Hello, Fat Boy."

Rising from the chair I walked toward my uncle, buried my face in his coat, and within seconds was choking back sobs. He patted my back and finally said, "My word, Fat Boy, I believe you've filled out there. You must have been drinking a lot of strawberry milk shakes." I tried to speak, but for a few minutes could only make choking sounds. When I found my voice I told him, no, I hadn't had a strawberry milk shake since he'd left, that I'd been lifting weights with the football team, that I was on all the kicking teams, and alternated every other series at defensive end.

"You wouldn't be pulling my leg now, would you, Fat Boy? I'd have never believed when I left Jefferson that you would ever have played in another football game. I'll never forget it, though you may not even remember it, but you were showing your daddy how you tackled a boy in the B-team game, and you shut your eyes and turned your head, and I never saw Floyd laugh so hard in my life. You're not trying to tackle them boys like that any more, are you?"

"No, I'm serious, Joe. I'm really playing now. I'll be playing tomorrow night. Say, why don't you come up to the game? It's homecoming and I know you won't believe this, but Peggy Jean is on the homecoming court."

"What do you mean? I can believe that. Your sister is a pretty girl. You don't know it because she's your sister."

"Try to come, Joe. It starts at eight o'clock."

He said he didn't know, but that he would try. It depended on what time the funeral was over and what all the family was doing after the funeral. "I can't make any promises," he said, "but if it works out that I can be there, I'll be there. Don't go looking for me, but if I'm there, I'll find you after the game."

"Come to where the team bus is down on the field. I'll look for you there," I said, unable to hide the excitement I felt.

"Alright, but remember I said I couldn't make any promises."

At the next morning's pep rally I told everyone who had ever known Joe that he might attend the night's game.

"No kidding!" said Smith. "Hadn't seen him in a while. Where's he been?"

"He said he's been up north. Ohio and Indiana. He was traveling around for a while. But he's back in Griffin now."

"Hope he comes. That'd be good."

"Joe?" Bill Elder said. "You let me know if he gets here. I'd sure like to see him. I know you'd love for him to see you play." He paused before adding, "It would be about the closest thing to having your Daddy there, wouldn't it?"

"Yeah," I nodded, tears welling in my eyes. "Yeah."

I hardly tasted the pregame steak and baked potato that afternoon. By five-thirty I was already dressed and lying on a mat in the weight room, silently pumping up adrenaline, preparing myself for the game as if it were a 210-pound bench press that must be attacked without distraction. By game time I was mentally psyched, so emotional as to be nearly in tears. I was ready.

There was little opportunity to prove myself during the game; our offense controlled the ball for long drives, keeping Hephzibah's offense and our defense off the field. When I did enter the game it was only for three plays, for we consistently shut them down and forced punts. Three plays from scrimmage, two kickoffs, and two punts were all I played the entire first half. The second half was much the same. After we'd scored a touchdown to take a 20–0 lead, the defense gave up a long touchdown drive while I shifted my weight impatiently from one foot to the other on the sideline. In the game's closing minutes, our offense scored another touchdown to put the game out of reach at 27–8.

"Kickoff team," Coach Lofton shouted, and we trotted to our positions. I lined up beside Coach Lofton's son, Jimmy, who was responsible for containment around the left end of our coverage. We tensed as the whistle blew, and when Simpson came forward to kick the ball I sprinted downfield in my lane, looking up to see which direction the ball was headed and where it would be caught—to my right, and at about the fifteen-yard line. Suddenly a squatty fellow wearing a red jersey, number sixty-four, seemed to appear from nowhere, knocking me off my feet. Rolling toward the sideline, I bounced up in time to see the return man dip outside Jimmy and streak down the sideline toward me. If he got past me, he would score.

Crouching, my head up, I stalked toward him, watching the boy's stomach. Joe must not see me fail. The boy ran closer, tried a feint inside, but I didn't take it. Putting my face on his stomach, I locked my arms, heard him grunt at the jolt, felt his body fall backward to the ground, heard the crowd's "Whooo!" My teammates pulled me from him, pounding my shoulder pads and helmet. "Good lick, Hoard. Good lick."

Stevie Underwood grabbed my helmet. "You nailed him, boy. You nailed him."

I grinned and said, "Some guy knocked the hell out of me."

He looked toward the return man walking groggily from the field and said, "Looks to me more like you knocked the hell out of him."

Minutes later the game ended with me on the field, spectators swarming across it, girls hugging my teammates, even hugging me. "Good game, Dickey," hollered my cousin, Al, who'd helped handle the yardsticks on the sideline. I waved and trotted over to him. "That was some lick on that kickoff. Probably the best lick I've seen all season."

"It felt good," I said, laughing and walking toward the bus before thinking to ask him, "Have you seen Joe?"

"Joe? You mean Joe Hoard? He supposed to be here?"

"Yeah. He said he would try to make it."

"No, I haven't seen him. If I do, I'll tell him you're looking for him."

The team bus had been parked across the track. The cars surrounding the bus formed shadows on the ground. I searched them for Joe. From behind me a hand grabbed my shoulder. I turned expectantly, only to see Jimmy Lofton. "Thanks," he said, sheepishly.

"Thanks for what?"

"You saved my butt out there on that kickoff. I got suckered inside there and he got around me."

"Well if some big hog hadn't knocked me out there, I'd have missed him, too," I said, thinking that Joe would be proud. He'd know better now than to think I would ever again turn my head and close my eyes to make a tackle, and so would my father. They'd both be proud. Elated, I searched the shadows, but Joe wasn't there; perhaps he'd planned on finding me back at the school. "Good game, Hoard," people said to me as we left the bus. "Let me shake your hand, sir," Benny Durden said. "One fine job on that kickoff."

At the school everyone filed off the bus and headed for the locker room to shower and dress for the homecoming dance next door in the cafeteria. I stood in the parking lot until everyone had gone, scanning the lot. But Joe never showed up.

My smile had long faded. I went to shower and dress, then made an appearance at the dance where my teammate warriors locked arms with steady girlfriends or those who would soon be; dance with the same girl twice in Jefferson, and everybody assumed you were practically married. I looked around the room and saw no prospects for a dancing partner. Bill Elder walked by with his arm around the shoulder of his date, his latest steady. "Hoard," he asked. "Did you ever hear from Joe?"

"Nah!" I said, shrugging. "Don't guess he could make it."

"That's too bad. You played a great game, buddy. I mean, you creamed that guy on that kickoff. I knew you were playing it for Joe. If he'd been here, he'd have been proud."

"Yeah, I reckon," I growled, walking away. Yeah, I had played that game for Joe, and in a sense for my father. But who was I kidding? My father was dead. And Joe was no longer a part of my life. They were both gone and would never be back. And all of my wishing them back didn't matter. I looked up at the cafeteria clock. Eleven-twenty-three. The dance would continue until midnight.

"No passes out," Miss Turpin said at the door.

"I know," I said. "I'm going home."

"Home? It's not even eleven-thirty. You're leaving the homecoming dance?"

"Yes, ma'am. I don't feel like staying. I'm tired."

The October air was brisk but not cold and despite my making the lick of the game and receiving the accolades that had followed, I felt a familiar restlessness as I walked alone toward the house. It was a pivotal moment in that I realized that the elation of achieving a dream doesn't last long—five or ten minutes at the most. There aren't enough people in the world who can say they love you often enough to make you start loving yourself, if you don't love yourself to begin with. And I realized that my heart would always ache for my father's approval. And that the shallow applause of people would not make him proud, not when he, a great athlete himself, had said, "there comes a time when you realize there are more important things in life than playing ball, son."

Chapter
Twenty-two

Boys wearing football jackets sat around me at the soda fountain of the drug store. In the booth behind us some girls wearing oversized senior rings fitted to their fingers by melted wax or rubber bands ventured toward the bounds of infidelity by flirting. Among them sat Elana Rosemont, a senior with chestnut hair and brown eyes swollen from tears; three days earlier her mother had died of cancer.

I wanted badly to sit in the booth beside her, put my arms around her, as I had done Sunday at her home shortly after Peggy Jean and I got the call that Mrs. Rosemont had died, but I couldn't because Maria Jensen sat beside her and, anyway, Elana wore one of those oversized rings. Months earlier when she had been between boyfriends and it had become obvious that her mother was dying, I had frequently telephoned her at night and for hours at a time we would talk about school, about our latest basketball game, about dreams for the future. It was friendly at first; she was too beautiful and popular for me to consider as a girlfriend, and I felt a curious lack of passion toward her, for she was too innocent, too virginal to lust after. But as the weeks passed my feelings had changed from friendship to tenderness. She was beautiful, not because of a voluptuous body, but because virtue seemed to emanate from her. And I wanted to hold her, be close, kiss her tenderly, be her hero. But after baiting her with some leading questions—"What do you think about dating someone younger? Would you date someone who couldn't drive?"—and hearing her response, "Just how young are you talking about," and telling her, "Someone my age—exactly," she had cut me short by telling me that she liked me but thought of me as a brother, to me the ultimate slur. Better that she hate me than to feel the indifference of a sibling. Hurt, I had telephoned her less frequently and soon she was wearing the ring she wore while fighting back tears in the drug-store booth. She dabbed at her eyes with a tissue, then blew her nose, and put the tissue in her purse. "Who are we playing this Friday night?" she asked, her lower lip quivering.

Truckie Myers, seated on a stool beside his girlfriend, answered: "We play Harlem."

"Nuh-uh," Elana said, suddenly giggling through a sob. "Y'all are teasing me."

"We most certainly do play Harlem Friday night."

"You mean—the Globetrotters?"

The boys howled with glee, Elana ducking her head in humiliation. "Yeah, we're playing the Harlem Globetrotters. Did you hear that? The Globetrotters."

"Y'all are mean," she said.

"But we really are playing Harlem."

"But they're not all—Negroes are they?"

Her question was greeted with more laughter. She tried to return to the boys' good graces by asking, "Will we beat them?"

"Of course we'll beat them," Truckie said. "You saw what we did to Hephzibah, didn't you? Coach Lofton said it was our best game so far. Even old Hoard over there played a good game."

"Nuh-uh," Elana objected. I cocked my head and glared at her. "Y'all are teasing me again."

"Did you hear that, Hoard. Elana there doesn't think you could play a good game."

"Dickey's not even on the football team," Elana stated to Truckie. In response to their laughter she corrected herself. "No, that's right. I guess I forgot you were playing. I'm sorry."

"Well, it's an honest mistake," said Truckie. "For a while there we didn't know if he was playing either."

"Y'all better lay off old Hoard," said Benny Durden. "He had the best lick of the game the other night."

"You, Dickey?" Maria Jensen was talking. "When was that?"

"The one on that last kickoff," said Benny. "The one right toward the end of the game. I mean he nailed that old boy."

"I don't remember. Oh, I guess we'd already gone back to the school." Maria, like Elana and Peggy Jean, had been on the homecoming court and had missed the play because they'd returned to the school to pose for photographs. Even the team's cameraman had shot a picture of the stadium lights on that last kickoff. Scowling, I sipped from my drink and turned toward the mirror.

"Look whose coming," Truckie said, eying the old man in the threadbare suit removing his hat as the door shut behind him. T.C. shuffled toward the soda fountain, frowning at the red football jackets. "Glad to see you, T.C. I've been wanting to ask you something." Truckie glanced around the room to see the approving grins. "Do you think Georgia Tech'll win any more football games this year? No, no, let me put it this way: Do you think Georgia Tech'll win any more games again—ever?"

The teenagers showed their appreciation for the question with approving snickers.

"They'll win at least one more game this year anyway," T.C. said, the boys responding in a cry of unison, "oh," the way they did whenever someone said fighting words.

"Oh, really, now. And just when do you think that might be?"

"They'll win when those Bulldogs come to Atlanta."

"Aw, come on, T.C. Georgia ain't sending their girls' team out there to play. They're sending the big boys."

"Quick as lightning, busy as bees,
Tech'll beat Georgia as much as they please."

"No, T.C. Those days are long gone."

T.C. haughtily shook his head as if the game had already been decided. "Tech'll figure out a way to outsmart 'em. And it won't take much to outsmart 'em."

"Sorry, T.C., but they're not allowed to take their slide rules out on the field. Just their manhood. And that's the problem. The Tech boys—if you can call 'em that—won't know whether to tackle our boys or feel them up."

"Y'all leave him alone," came the pleading cry from Elana.

"Leave him alone? All I did was ask him one little question."

T.C. stepped past them and halted beside me, raising two fingers. "Me and you, Georgia Tech," he said.

The room fell silent. Clenching my jaw, I turned away, looking in the mirror, aware of the grinning faces anticipating my response. Truckie Myers spoke. "I've told you before, T.C., and I'll tell you again. Old Hoard's not for Tech any more. He's for Georgia."

The old man tapped my shoulder. "Me and you, Georgia Tech," he said. I looked over at Truckie and Benny and the others watching with eyebrows raised. Why didn't they leave the old man alone? And why didn't they leave me alone?

"Me and you, Georgia Tech," he said again, tapping my shoulder. Suddenly, I brushed his hand away and stared at him, seeing for a moment his bewildered and hurt expression before I shouted, "Go Dawgs." He scurried from the drug store without so much as a glance back.

"Hot'll mighty! Did you see that? Old T.C. looked like he was gonna die."

Looking around the room I saw the flushed face of Elana Rosemont, the snickers of Truckie and Benny and others. I knew at the time that had none of them been present I simply would have raised my hand to T.C. and said, "Me and you." But to save face with them I had hurt an innocent man, whose only crime was to choose a different team.

"Y'all are mean," Elana Rosemont said. But I knew I was worse than mean. I was a coward.

Chapter
Twenty-three

The smirk I wore as T.C. tramped from the drug store that afternoon belied the regret I felt at betraying him. The pride I'd felt the past two weeks had been replaced by a pit in my stomach, a sense of shame. While listening to the howls of raucous laughter, I recognized that not only had I gained the status of football player, but the conceit and arrogance as well. I had become what once I had hated. And hated what I had become.

For the rest of the season, my play lacked intensity. Having proved that I could play, my need to play had been enervated. The anger was still with me, I know. But it was tired.

Truckie Myers's prophecy of easy victory over Harlem Friday night proved false. We struggled to a scoreless tie. Saturday night, I rode to a dance hall outside Athens with Woody Herbert and Todd Brown, who, now that I'd proven myself a genuine football player, condescended to risk being seen with me. Though our first efforts at conversation had proved awkward, after a couple of beers we became more at ease; alcohol seemed not only to improve my own personality but also Todd Brown's.

Looking back, I recall that Todd had plenty to be bitter about: he had injured his knee the previous spring practice and would never play football again; his own father had been killed in an airplane crash when Todd was about six years old. But despite that commonality, we were still five years away from any discussion of our fathers.

Most likely, Todd believed, as did I, that it was unmanly to do anything other than what growing up on Jefferson's athletic fields had taught us to do, "to suck it up and go," because "when the going gets tough, the tough get going," as if life were all one big football game played fairly by all sides.

And so when sober, Todd's normal demeanor was a stolid sneer. But after a couple of beers the curled lip relaxed into a silly grin and his scoffs became laughter. A few beers helped to unite our hearts in condemning much of the world to hell, accusing many of its occupants of either a canine ancestry or no traceable paternal lineage at all, even provided the courage to enter a darkened room to dance with some girl neither of us would have been caught dead with in the light of day.

After a few songs, we got our hands stamped before sneaking out for another can of courage. I wanted to get drunk. No, I wanted to be happy, but had no idea how to be happy without the help of chemistry. Inspired by my third beer I roved about the dance hall, shaking hands with strangers and telling them that I was Dick Nixon and would appreciate their vote in Tuesday's election.

Most people seemed to enjoy the buffoonery: "Yeah, Tricky Dicky, you've got my vote," they would say, shaking my hand so vigorously that I began to suspect my future might lie in politics; there seemed little more to it than thinking yourself important and acting happy to meet the voters. Grinning broadly, I left one cluster of admirers to find myself staring into the soft eyes of a girl who'd suddenly stepped from the crowd to shake my hand. "Hi," I said. "I'm Dick Nixon and I'd appreciate your vote."

Her smile faded. She looked at me like Maria Jensen had looked at Jim the first day he hobbled on crutches into algebra class after spraining his ankle, as if she were peering into a lover's coffin. Were the tears welling up in these angelic eyes for me? Had this girl somehow peered into my soul to see how closely I had tottered near catastrophe, how much I wanted to love and be loved? Marveling at her beauty, the brown hair to her shoulders, her moist lips shaded with pink lipstick, I stood paralyzed, my grin twisting into a stare of awe and worship. She stepped toward me, her chin rising as she kissed my lips, briefly, sweetly. Clearing the cobwebs from my head, I turned toward the exit before halting in my tracks, chastising myself for retreating before finding out her name, her address. I turned again toward her, but she was gone. I pressed through the crowd, straining through the darkness, wondering how she could have disappeared so quickly.

"Where'd that girl go?" I asked someone.

"What girl?"

"The girl who kissed me?"

"Some girl kissed you? Then what are you doing talking to me."

"I don't know where she went."

"Well, if she kissed you, Tricky Dicky, she'll probably vote for you," the boy laughed.

But I was no longer interested in the joke. I moved through the crowd, looking for her. Perhaps she had stepped outside. Suddenly I felt a tug at my shoulder. "Come on, Dickey," Woody Herbert said. "We've got to get out of here. You're gonna get our butts locked up."

"I'm alright, Herbert, I swear. There's this girl—"

"I ain't kidding you, man, we've got to get out of here right now. Everybody is talking about you."

"Wait, Herbert, I've got to find this girl."

"We can't wait. Here, give me your sweater."

"Why?"

"Just give me your sweater."

Reluctantly I removed the white basketball sweater, and Herbert folded it and tucked it beneath his jacket. He and Todd led me outside, warning me to walk straight as we passed by two policemen who leaned against the building. "Keep moving and don't look back," Herbert said beneath clenched teeth. When we reached the car, Woody practically shoved me inside, and Todd sped away, breathing more easily and looking less often in the rearview mirror as we crossed the Jackson County line.

"I want my sweater," I said. "Why'd you take my sweater?"

"Because the police, man, were looking for a boy in a white basketball sweater with the big J on it. All you had to do was walk outside wearing that and your ass would have been locked up."

"For what?"

"For public drunk."

"Oh, I wasn't really drunk. I was just having fun."

"Well then, how about underaged drinking? That's reason enough to lock you up."

"Y'all, there was this girl. She kissed me."

"Damn, Hoard, she was probably some narc smelling your breath and running straight to the law. We're lucky we're not all in jail."

The next two Saturdays I returned with Woody and Todd, staying sober, hoping for the girl's entry, disappointed that she never showed up. Once basketball season started, most weekend nights were tied up with games, so nearly a month passed before I could return wearing a new football jacket, having earned my varsity letter. Looking around the darkened room hazy with smoke and echoing with the band's rendition of "My Girl," I grew depressed. My girl wasn't among the dancers leaning against one another during the slow song or among the girls leaning against the wall.

"She had brown hair," I told Herbert for about the fourth time. "About to her shoulders."

"Damn, Hoard," Woody shouted. "Give it up? A dozen girls in here have brown hair to their shoulders. You've got to tell me more than that. How old was she? Did she have any birthmarks? Any scars? Did she have all her teeth? Did she have any teeth? Did she have big—"

"It wasn't like that, Herbert."

"She was either a narc, Hoard, or some hooker trying to make a quick ten."

"I don't think so."

On the concrete floor, couples intoxicated by the aphrodisiac of music embraced and smiled dreamily, girls gazing into their lover's eyes or snuggling cheek to shoulder.

"Slim pickings here tonight," yelled Herbert above the din. "Good thing those girls are all inside."

"Why's that?"

"If they were outside they'd all be howling at the moon."

I sniggered and said, "Maybe it's just early. I think I'm going out for a while."

Near the front door stood some boys from Jefferson, older boys who most likely possessed a six pack or two. I approached one who told me, no, he didn't have any beer, but that I could probably buy some from a boy named Tom. "No," said Tom, "but I think I can find us one. I could use one myself."

I watched his movement around the room, his behind-the-hand questions to those who shook their heads in reply until finally a college boy nodded, removed car keys from a pocket and swapped them for a pair of one dollar bills. "Come on," Tom said, and I followed him outside, walking past the two policemen leaning against the wall near the entrance, moving past the vehicles parked throughout the lot until we reached a car where Tom inserted a key into the trunk, opened it, and removed two bottles of beer from the six-pack carton. He put the bottles beneath his coat and we walked to his own car where we sat inside on the front seat and opened the bottles to release the smell of lukewarm beer. We had taken no more than a few sips before Tom straightened up in the driver's seat and peered out through the windshield. "Uh-oh," he said.

"What?"

"Look!" he said, staring across the parking lot toward the dance hall. "They know what we're up to."

"Who?"

"The cops."

Then I saw them, two policemen, perhaps fifty yards away, walking with purpose toward us. Unable to disguise the fear in my voice, I asked, "What do we do?"

"Just set your bottle on the side of the car."

"Outside?"

"No. No, between the seat and the door. They won't be able to see it there."

Trembling, afraid I'd drop the bottle from the car instead of placing it where Tom had said, I set the beer in front of the seat, opened the door, jumped from the car and locked the door behind me. As Tom and I walked toward the building the two policemen met us. "Good evening, sirs," Tom said, smiling. The policemen said nothing, one of them removing a flashlight from his belt as he walked toward the car. Turning I could see him shining a beam of light through the windshield. Tom kept his pace toward the dance hall until one policeman said, "Here it is. Right here," and hollered, "Hey, you boys, stop it right there."

"Who? Us?" Tom asked, shrugging, his palms turned up as if annoyed.

"That's right. Both of you." The policemen walked toward us, pulling another object from his belt. My God, was it a gun? No, handcuffs.

My knees buckled.

"Yessir, can I help you?" Tom asked.

"You fellows drinking beer?"

"Oh, no sir," Tom said, shaking his head. But I knew I'd been caught and that lying would make it worse and so I said, "Yessir," ignoring Tom's incredulous scowl. "Yessir, I was."

"Well, at least you're honest. Maybe you two boys would like to come with us for a while." He stepped toward me, holding out the handcuffs. I leaned against a car for support. "Stand up straight, young man. That is, if you can."

"Yessir."

"I believe spending a night downtown with us is just what you two boys need," the older policeman said.

My head reeled. What would Mama say? And Coach Knight. "Please, sir, don't. I'll—I'll get kicked off the basketball team."

"Too bad you didn't think of that before now. You boys will really have your eyes opened up after a night with us."

A night with them! A night spent in a jail cell smelling of stale urine and puke. Rats and roaches and winos and queers. I supported myself against the car. "Aw, officer," Tom said, smiling. "There's no need for that. We haven't created a disturbance. And I'm nineteen years old."

"How old are you, son?" the older policeman asked.

"Sixteen."

"Well, then," he said, turning back toward Tom. "Looks like you have supplied a minor, doesn't it?"

"I didn't know he was just sixteen."

"Why are you getting us?" I asked. "Why don't you get all the drunks inside?" I knew the remark sounded stupid almost the moment I said it.

"All the drunks inside, son? All the drunks inside? Why I think we're doing pretty good at getting them outside."

"Don't lock us up," Tom pleaded. "We were just getting one beer."

"That's all anybody ever drinks at a time. But one beer leads to another, doesn't it, son?"

"Yes, sir. You're right about that," Tom said, laughing at the policeman's wit. "Alright then, look, I'm the one that bought the beer. You can take me and lock me up. But this fellow here ain't never been in any trouble. It would mess him up pretty bad."

"Always a first time for getting in trouble, isn't it, son?" He was speaking to me.

"Yessir," I gasped, suddenly nauseated. If I puked he'd think I was drunk for sure.

"Stand up straight, son. For saying you had only one beer, you sure are having a hard time supporting yourself."

"He's just scared, officer."

A crowd had gathered about twenty yards away, among them Herbert and Todd, keeping their distance to avoid any guilt by association. "Alright, son," said the older policeman. "Go get the beer." Reeling, I walked toward the car, so conscious about walking a straight line that I stumbled against the door. "It's locked," I said. Tom opened the door for me and I removed the beer.

"Get both of them, son," the older policeman said. Fearful of his command to pick up the evidence against me, humiliated before the onlookers who leered at me as if they'd never touched a beer in their lives, I carried the bottle to the policeman. "Now, son, pour that beer out on the ground."

"Right here?"

"No. Don't stink up these folks's pavement. Take it over to the grass."

I walked to the curbing and knelt to pour out the beer which left a puddle of foam in the earth, not looking up toward those watching from a distance.

"Stand up."

Shaking, I turned and faced the policeman. "Now, listen to me," he said. "I won't take you in this time, but if I ever see you down here again with any beer, I'll put you in the jail so fast it'll make your head spin. What I want you to do right now is to have this boy take you straight home."

"I'm with some other boys."

"You didn't come down here with this boy?"

"No sir."

"These other boys drinking beer, too."

"No, sir, just me."

"Well, you go find those boys and tell them I said to get you straight home. You understand?"

Herbert and Todd had already begun walking through the parking lot. They never looked back, but went straight to the car and sat in the front seat. When I slipped into the back seat, Herbert turned to me. "Hoard, do you know how close you came to getting your ass thrown in jail?"

"I could see the headlines in tomorrow's paper," sneered Todd. "Jefferson's star basketball player arrested for public drunk."

"You know what, Todd? We're gonna have to quit hanging around with this guy. He's gonna ruin our reputations."

"No offense, Hoard, but it'll be a cold day in July before I bring you back down here again."

"That's okay," I said, before settling into a morose silence for the remainder of the ride home. "I don't think I'm ever coming back." And I never did.

Chapter
Twenty-four

Basketball games were scheduled for nearly every weekend night through February, leaving me little time for the diversions of alcohol. But after the season I spent many Friday and Saturday evenings with Marcus, whose enrichments at the University of Georgia had included developing a taste for cheap beer. At college he enjoyed a can or two each evening in his trailer, at home he drank in his Mustang. "Just drive forty-five and keep to the back roads and nobody'll mess with you," he said. Splitting a six pack with Marcus soon became my Friday reward for surviving another week of school. It was all I cared about. My schoolwork suffered. I failed trigonometry for the quarter, seemed destined to fail it for the year, and my grade in chemistry was a D. At least my grades in English and literature were good. Our teacher, a young woman named Mrs. Case, was making us read the existentialists and the romantics. And while others struggled with "Thanatopsis," dismissing such poetry as stupid ("it doesn't even rhyme"), I seemed to find kindred spirits in the likes of William Cullen Bryant, who at age seventeen wrote:

> and what if thou withdraw
> in silence from the living; and no friend
> Take note of thy departure? All that breathe
> Will share thy destiny. The gay will laugh
> When thou art gone, the solemn brood of care

Plod on, and each one, as before, will chase
His favorite phantom; yet all these shall leave
Their mirth and their employments, and shall come
And make their bed with thee. . . .

When Bryant wrote his poem in 1811 he must have been sur-
rounded by silly and shallow girls batting their eyes at some boy
whose quest for true love had included purchasing his first carriage or
winning some horserace, all of them, the studious and the slothful,
the manly and the sissy, the popular and the ignored, all walking at
their chosen paces on their chosen pathways to the graveyard, none
of them giving a thought to dying until their hour to taste it.

"The Epicureans," said Mrs. Case, "had a philosophy: 'Eat, drink,
and be merry, for tomorrow we die.' They thought that the purpose
in life was to have pleasure."

"Sounds good to me," said Big Ed, stirring from his daily struggle
to keep awake after lunch.

"The trouble with that is that pleasure has its laws of diminishing
returns; hand holding is exciting for a while, but after it gets old, it
takes a greater stimulus to create an equal amount of pleasure."

I suspected she was right. A couple of beers used to get me pleasantly drunk. Now they just gave me a warm glow. But the trouble
with her line of thinking was that one must allow for the possibility that even sex could get old, something one unwillingly pristine
could not even pretend to believe. Not while leering at the passionate
Mrs. Case, presiding before the class. She was in her twenties, her
face unblemished but too thin and pale. She wore deep red lipstick
and had perfect teeth, so that on the rare occasion when she genuinely smiled, she was radiant. Some days I wished I could bury my
face into her shoulder and have her embrace me. I wanted her approval. When she gave me an A-plus for a short story about a father's
return from the grave to avenge his son's taking his death too lightly
I glowed for days. She took an interest in me and tried to involve me
in class discussions. "And what do you think the poet meant by the
'music unheard,' Dickey?" she asked one day as we studied "Ode on

a Grecian Urn.' " " 'Heard melodies are sweet, but those unheard are sweeter. . . . '?"

"Dickey?"

"Mmm," I groaned. "I don't know."

"Oh, I think you do. Anyone who can write the stories you do knows something about imagination."

Sighing and shifting in my seat, I cleared my throat and said, "Well, sometimes something may look pretty good to you, and you think you may want it . . ."

When I faltered she prodded me along. "Something idyllic?"

"Yeah, and when you get there, it isn't what you think. The music is—well—off key."

"Then what you imagine can be more pleasant than what you actually experience?"

I thought of the nameless girl who kissed me at the dance hall and vanished, leaving me with reveries of moonlit strolls and soft kisses when in reality she might have been exactly as Herbert had said, a hooker who would accept my sacrifice of innocence and ten dollars in exchange for the clap. "I guess what you imagine is usually better."

"Maybe it's better that the fair youth of whom Keats says 'never, never canst thou kiss, though winning near the goal,' " never does get to kiss the girl."

"She might have bad breath," quipped Smith.

"Exactly," said the perfect Mrs. Case. "Real people have their faults."

"Yeah," said Con Underwood. "Here is this simple picture of the past where everyone is happy and young and it isn't real at all. It probably never was as perfect as the picture painted on the urn."

"But," said Mrs. Case. "Aren't people always creating illusions. Tell me, is it easier to imagine that once upon a time you were really happy, or that one day you hope to be happy, than to be happy right now? Aren't most of us always saying, "If I could only have this, or if I could only go back to a particular time, then I would be happy?"

Yes, I thought, I had said it, somehow convincing myself that life had somehow been better before my father had been killed, and when

George was alive. That life had been simpler and happy and that, could I somehow have been transported back in time, then I would be happy. But there had never been a time when life was completely happy. Even a little child has his day ruined by a burned finger or a bee sting or a spanking. Brooding, I withdrew from the discussion, unwilling to say what I thought.

"Mysterious," Mrs. Case described me to the whole class one afternoon during a session on adjectives. After one-word summaries of various students, she had turned toward me with a particular relish. "I don't think there is a person in this room who knows the real Dickey Hoard. I don't think any of you know how deep his thoughts are. Most of you would be surprised if you knew what he was thinking."

Mrs. Case certainly would have been surprised to know how frequently she was the object of my fantasies. Would she be shocked to learn how I loved her? No, she would be amused. She would laugh. She wished to understand me, not because she cared about me, but so she could better handle me. Well, if the lovely Mrs. Case thought she could handle me, then my prolonged silences were vindicated. Let her only guess at what I thought. Let her be frustrated at her inability to understand me.

"Look at me, Dickey," she said to me one afternoon after I'd answered a question with an "I don't know."

"Look at me, Dickey. You do know. Tell me what you're thinking."

"I'm not thinking anything," I replied, scowling, crossing my arms and staring down at my desk where the names of scholars past had been etched for posterity.

"No, look at me. Don't look down. I'm talking to you. When someone is talking to you, you look at them. See, there you go again. Don't look down. Look at me."

I glanced up at her, my teeth clenched in subdued rage. She said, "What are you hiding?"

"Nothing," I growled, looking back down at my desktop.

"Then look at me. What are you thinking?"

She would have had me expelled had I told her that I wanted to pin her down and wipe the red lipstick right off her face and strip her as naked as she was trying to strip me. I wanted to rape her at knifepoint and then kiss away her tears, except that she probably would have stopped me to tell me I was doing the whole thing wrong. I hated her with a passionate love.

"Why is it that when you find someone you love it's always someone out of your reach?" I asked Marcus as we rode the back roads one Saturday afternoon.

"Believe me," Marcus replied. "I've asked myself that question a thousand times. You'd almost believe there really was a Cupid flying around shooting arrows into your heart, making you act smitten. Some force beyond yourself. You try to tell yourself, 'I am not in love with this girl,' but damn it all, you know you are, and you hate yourself for it. Why can't I just forget about her? After what she's done, I ought to hate her, but I don't."

"You're talking about Elana Rosemont?"

"Exactly," he said. "You know I was supposed to have a date with her last night," he said.

"What do you mean, 'supposed to'?"

"She was supposed to go with me to the concert in Athens. But she phoned me about an hour before I was leaving to pick her up. I mean, I was bathed and dressed when the phone rang and she told me she couldn't go, that she was sick and her daddy wanted her to stay home. So there I was, stuck with these two tickets to the concert, so I figured, what the hell, I'd ask my brother if he wanted to go, so there I am at this concert with my little brother, and at intermission, I go to get a Coke and who do you think I happen to run into?"

"Elana?"

"Not exactly. But close enough. I ran into her date."

"I can't believe it."

"I couldn't believe it either. Seems like if she was going to lie to me, she would at least have enough sense to stay clear of the very place I'd invited her to."

"What did she say?"

"Oh, she didn't see me. But I sure as hell saw her. I watched Walter go back to his seat. And sure enough, as sure as I'm sitting here, there she was in the lovely flesh."

"And you sit here talking about loving her?"

"I told you I couldn't help it. I hate her and want to slap her face and cuss her out, but I can't help it, I still love her. And hate myself for loving her."

"You mean, you'd ask her out again?"

"No, I didn't say that. I may never ask anybody out again. Speak of the devil."

Elana Rosemont in her father's light blue Plymouth had circled out of the parking lot of the bowling alley. Smiling, I waved to her and motioned for her to drive back into the lot. "What are you doing, Hoard? I don't have anything to say to her right now."

"Well, I do," I said, rolling down the car window and inviting Elana to park her car and sit in the Mustang with us. She smiled shyly and consented, walking toward my side of the car. I got out, lifting up the backrest of the front seat, and once she was in, I set it back, trapping her in the back seat. "How are you Elana?"

"Fine," she said, smiling back at me.

"I mean how are you feeling? I heard you'd been sick."

Her smile faded. "I'm fine," she said. "I'm doing better."

"You mean better than you were last night. Because I heard you were mighty sick. You were too sick to go out on a date with Marcus last night."

"That's right," she said. Her face did seem pale and her lower lip was quivering. "But I'm better. I felt well enough to come to town."

"Actually," I said with a sneer. "You were well enough to go to the concert last night. In fact, you did go to the concert last night, didn't you?"

Her mouth fell open, her face turned pink, her eyes moist. She tried to speak, but said nothing, and looked at the back of Marcus's head. I snickered at the virtuous Elana, a transgressor after all. "Elana, you look a little surprised to hear that. I guess you didn't figure on Marcus seeing you there last night, did you?"

She said nothing, blinking back tears. "You know what, Elana, I really thought you were different. I hoped you were different. But you're no different than other girls, Elana. You know what you are? A bitch. A real bitch."

As the tears streamed down her face, I jeered and lifted up the seat. "You can go now," I said. "I just thought you'd like to know that you're one bitch who got caught playing her little games."

Chapter
Twenty-five

I suppose that what I said to Elana Rosemont was what I'd also wanted to say to Mrs. Case and a list of other females. Elana just happened to ride by in the blue Plymouth at the wrong time. Or maybe my abusing Elana had something to do with anticipatory grief; within the month she would graduate and join the growing list of those who'd left and forgotten me. Of course I would have preferred for Elana Rosemont and Mrs. Case to love me rather than hate me, but better that they hate me than forget me.

With Peggy Jean soon to graduate and the approaching summer marking the second anniversary of my father's death, I felt fresh waves of grief. Time would heal all wounds, people had told me. They said grief would pass. But time brought new milestones and milestones reminded me of my father's absence: he would not be there to see Peggy Jean in cap and gown. During the day, I could push such thoughts aside, but at night, Daddy used milestones to invade my dreams. Two themes recurred, one of impending holocaust. The Russians launch a nuclear missile, air raid sirens wail, frantic people scurry for bomb shelters. My father, wearing a coat and tie and a serene smile, passively observes, almost amused by the chaos. I run to him for help, and he smiles and I stand there beside him as he peacefully watches the world rush toward doom. The second dream was of my father grabbing up his keys, walking toward his car, oblivious to my silent screams and my heavy-footed efforts to chase him down. He sits in the car, waves to me, smiling and serene, as I plead in horror for him not to crank the car, and only when he turns the ignition do I wake up trembling, set to spend the day at school in silent anger.

Three weeks remained in the school year. When the school bell sounded release for the second weekend in May, I went to the gym hoping to find that a few boys had stayed around for a pickup game of basketball. But everybody had gone, and after shooting baskets alone for a while, I walked home, plotting my evening; Marcus would be in Jefferson for the weekend and together we could cruise the back roads and drink a few beers. I looked in my wallet. Six dollars. And tomorrow I'd receive another check from the clothing store where for the past few months I had been working on Saturdays.

At 4:30 I walked in the back screened door, surprised to hear grease popping in a skillet of fried chicken and see the lid dancing on a pot of green beans. "What are y'all cooking so early for?" I asked.

Ignoring my question Mama demanded to know where I'd been.

"The same place I've been every day this week; at the gym shooting baskets. What's the big deal?"

"Well, get on over to the church. I told them you would be there right after school to help them move some tables for the church supper tonight."

"Church supper? It's Friday!"

"It's that lay mission whatchacallit they've been talking about the past three months. Where have you been, son?"

I suppressed the urge to retort that of all the places I'd been the last three months, church was not one of them. Instead, I said, "I'll help, but you ought not tell people what I'm going to do. You're lucky I'm not still playing basketball at the gym."

Walking across the street, I entered in the back door of the stone building, where the new preacher, Reverend Berry, spotted me and grabbed my hand. "Here's some good strong help right here," he said to a few teenaged boys I'd never seen before. The boys, who had done most of the work already, offered handshakes and introduced themselves. They were Baxter and Freddy and they were from Atlanta, seniors on next year's Avondale High School football team, and they had come to Jefferson for the weekend as part of the Lay Witness Mission. "Well I hope you have a good time," I said. After helping them move a few tables and a dozen or two chairs to the church annex, I turned to leave and saw a gray-haired man with a gap-toothed smile holding out his hand toward me.

"You're a member of this church here, aren't you?" he asked.

"I guess you could say that."

"Good. I was looking for someone to represent your youth at our opening meeting."

I fidgeted, clearing my throat. "Well, I think you're probably looking for Jim Smith or Con Underwood."

"But none of them are here, and we want at least one young person from this church at our meeting. I think you could represent them just fine."

"How long a meeting?"

"Thirty-minutes or so. At the most an hour."

"Oh—I don't know," I said, trying not to recoil visibly. "I guess I could do that."

I followed him to an upstairs room where chairs had been placed in a circle. A couple of adults from our church, eyebrows raised in mild surprise at my appearance, nodded at me. Two grown men, strangers to me, hugged each other in greeting. Horrified, I sat quickly and crossed my arms, watching Freddy pass out mimeographed song sheets and Baxter remove from its case—a guitar! I wondered how our church people were taking this. If Miss Lucy Wilborne were present she might usher these boys right out of this holy church house. I glanced at my watch. Ten minutes after five. I stared down at the paper, mumbling along as if really trying to learn the song. Should I fake a coughing attack, get up and leave for a drink of water and escape? No, it was too obvious. Where were Jim Smith or Con Underwood? Where were the girls who always came to church? Someone had warned them. But here I was trapped into singing like some pissant choir boy. Baxter finished the song and started another. "Kum Ba Ya, my Lord. Kum Ba Ya. . . ." I stole another glance at my watch. Good Lord! Eleven minutes after five!

After the songs, each person was called upon to give his name and hometown and why he had come, some of them having come from distant towns with their entire families, others alone, all of them to my surprise having appeared in Jefferson, they said, because they wanted to. Finally all eyes fell on me. I shifted uncomfortably and said, "My name is Dickey Hoard and I live across the street."

Encouraged by some approving chuckles, I continued. "I'm here because I was downstairs moving chairs and got invited to this meeting." I flushed at their laughter, amazed that these people seemed unopposed to humor in the house of God. Before the meeting ended, the leader asked us to stand and hold the hand of the person next to us, which wasn't too bad because I had taken a seat between two girls, one who kept squeezing my hand through the prayer, especially when she herself prayed as if she thought God was actually standing in the room with us, instead of up in the sky somewhere. Finally they dismissed and I hurriedly ducked down the stairwell and escaped to the house where I asked Mammie to cook me some hot dogs.

"Doll-boy, you heard your mama say we're all gonna eat supper over at the church tonight."

"I'd rather just eat a hot dog here."

Mama entered the kitchen just in time to hear the remark. "If you're going to eat supper tonight, you'll eat it at the church."

"That's what you think," I muttered, leaving the room and shutting the door behind me, stopping at the telephone in the hall to dial Bill Elder's number. His mother answered. "Excuse me, you'll have to speak up."

"Is Bill there?"

"Oh, hello, Dickey. No he's not here. He's gone off to spend the night."

I dialed Andrew's number. He wasn't home. Gus had a date. Jim would be at the church. I cursed my luck and returned to the kitchen to avow that just because I was eating supper at the church didn't mean I planned on staying half the night there for any meeting.

Within the hour, Mama announced that she was ready to leave and that I should hurry so that I could walk across the street with the entire family. I locked myself in the bathroom until my little sisters grew impatient and whined for Mama to take them on. She hollered to me that she'd better see me at the church in five minutes, and walked out the door. I came out of the bathroom and from the front door watched them walk across the street, Claudine pressing ahead, Vivian clinging to Mammie, Peggy Jean lagging behind no more enthusiastic about the prospects for her Friday night than was I. Walk with them? Mama had a better chance of freezing a snowball in hell than have me be seen crossing the street with them.

Fifteen minutes later I walked across the street and found Marcus leaning over the cast-iron fence reading the words on William Martin's tomb.

"Remember, man, as you walk by,
As you are now. . . ."

"Marcus," I said. "What are you doing here?"

"Believe me, I'm asking myself the very same question. I walked in the door this evening expecting some of Mama's home cooking and was informed, no, rather, I was told I'd be eating supper at the church. I don't know what kind of crap this is, but I've got better things to do than spend my Friday night at church like some tag-along child."

"I figured you'd be riding the back roads tonight."

"That's exactly where I'm headed just as soon as I eat."

"You waiting to eat?"

"Oh, yeah, I'll eat. You can't go wrong eating at a covered dish supper. It'll be the best food my stomach has seen this week. And besides, the price is right. But you see that car right there?" he asked, pointing at the white Mustang. "After supper, you'll see my ass sitting in it and headed right around the corner."

"Can I go with you?"

"Just meet me at the car after we eat. But don't expect me to wait around. First chance I get, I'm out of here."

My spirits lifted. A chance for a few beers. Friday night would not be lost after all. I gorged down fried chicken and ham, deviled eggs and potato salad, baked beans and corn, twice cleaning my plate before following Marcus to the kitchen to dispose of our trash. "Dickey," Dot said, accosting me. "You can do me a big favor if you cleaned out my banana pudding. I sure don't want to take any back home."

There was at the bottom of the bowl a generous helping of pudding, the soggy vanilla wafers having broken and combined with custard to form a paste covering a few bites of banana. The meringue had been eaten but meringue was my least favorite part. Accepting the offer, I finished the contents before looking up for Marcus. He was gone. I set down the bowl and pressed through the crowd. One of the church members grabbed my arm. "Look at you, Dickey. It's hard for me to believe how much you've filled out. You'll be making lots of tackles for us this year on our football team."

"Yessir," I said. "I've been lifting weights. Sorry, but I've got to catch up with Marcus."

I finally reached the door and opened it to look for Marcus. He had cranked the white Mustang and was driving off. As I leaped out the door to chase him, the gray-haired man with the gap tooth turned in my pathway. "Dickey," he said, "you're planning on meeting upstairs with us, aren't you?"

"Uh—yessir," I said, my heart sinking as the gears of the Mustang shifted and the car turned the corner to freedom. Angry, I followed the other teenagers like a herd of nursery students to the same upstairs room I'd been trapped in earlier, killing a Friday night playing games and singing songs, once drawing an ugly glare from Baxter when I sang improvised lyrics. When finally released, I thought the worst of the weekend had ended. But I was wrong. Mama stood at the foot of the stairs talking to Reverend Berry, who had Freddy by the shoulder, "Be glad to. Dickey's got a room to himself now," she was saying, "and he's got the bunk beds plus his own bed. We'll be glad to keep him."

"Damn," I muttered. Was this some kind of conspiracy? All I wanted, after spending a whole week racking my brains in school, tackling cosines and Henry David Thoreau and World War II, was two or three hours of relief drinking a few beers. And here not only was my Friday night ruined, but my entire weekend. I stepped outside to conceal my irritation in privacy only to find myself accosted by one of the visiting teenaged girls, balancing on the roots of an ancient oak. She called me by name.

"I'm impressed." I said.

She smiled and asked, "At what?"

"You remembered my name."

"Do you remember mine?" she asked, her head down but her eyes looking up toward me playfully.

"I'm sorry. No."

"It's Jenni. Are you going to be here tomorrow?"

I shook my head. "No, I have to work."

"Oh," she said as if genuinely disappointed. "Well, when do you go to work?"

"About eight-thirty. Store opens at nine."

"When do you get off?"

"At six."

"We'll still be here at six."

"Well," I stammered. "Sometimes I might have to work late. By the time I get in and eat supper, it could be seven-thirty—even later."

"We'll be here as late tomorrow night as we are tonight." I glanced at my watch to see that it was after nine-thirty and looked back at Jenni to see her grinning at me. I couldn't help but grin back at her persistence. But my grin faded when Mama emerged from the church to order me to help Freddy carry his bags to our house. "See you tomorrow night?" Jenni asked.

I had no idea what this lay mission thing was all about. All I knew was that I wanted no part of it, that I felt enough demands on me from teachers and coaches, enough expectations of me from Mama and Mammie and friends, to consider letting anyone else, even God, plant a hook in me and take away the slim pleasures found in drinking a few beers. And besides, if there was a God, I saw little evidence that He'd ever done anything for me.

"Maybe I'll see you," I told Jenni. "But I kind of doubt it."

Chapter
Twenty-six

At my job the next afternoon I picked up straight pins from beneath a row of shirts and tried to quash the strange feeling of disquietude. I felt as if something were wrong, as if I'd forgot some major test or project at school. There was an English paper due, but not until next Friday, still plenty of time. What was bothering me I couldn't say. Was it one of those compulsions that had sometimes resulted in my phoning whatever girl had next come to mind in hopes that a spark of passion might be ignited? Was some girl causing me such restlessness?

"You sure have been quiet today," the store owner said. "Are you feeling alright?"

"Yes, sir, I feel fine. Just got my mind on school, I guess."

"Did I tell you that your mother phoned awhile ago? Something about a meeting at your church. Wanted to know if I'd let you off. I told her it would be fine."

The two other salesmen rolled their eyes at the mention of church and leaned forward to hear my reply. "No, sir," I said. "I'll just go ahead and work."

But as the afternoon crawled by, the strange urging persisted until finally I suspected that my uneasiness had something to do with what was happening at the church. Something about it—was it curiosity?—made me want to return. Was it the girl who had squeezed my hand during that prayer? No, she was not a prospect for the back

...d he robbing the cradle. My disquietude
... event? I didn't know. By five
... the store owner in

"Going to the ...
Looking around to ma... ...
ventured near the door, I mumbled, ...
"You go ahead. It's a slow day."

After he counted up my hours and wrote me a check, ...
home, weary, not so much from work, but from life. I was tired of
being angry, tired of hating, tired of trying to be someone other than
myself to please others. A few beers would snap me out of the fatigue,
I thought. But only for an hour or two. I'd only wake up feeling
depressed again. I didn't know what I wanted, except maybe to be
honest and admit that I was tired of being a phony who played out
his life before all the wrong audiences, always worried about what
everyone else was thinking about me, doing everything from playing
football to struggling in the classroom trying to win the approval of
others, when even if I did win their approval, what had I really won?
No, I didn't want to drink beer tonight. But what else was there to
do in Jefferson except play ball or drink beer? Go to church? The
phoniest place I'd ever been in my life? Lord, I thought, so it had
come down to this.

I parked the car at Mammie's and didn't even bother to go in the
house. Mama might be there and she might tell me to go to church,
and if she did, so help me God I'd get in the car and ride off to
get myself knee-walking drunk. It was my choice to walk across this
street, though why I would choose to, I didn't know. As good an explanation as any came from Jenni, when she saw me turn the corner
and stared at me as if I'd arrived by strolling across the Oconee River
instead of Martin Street. "Dickey," she exclaimed. "You came back.
We were praying for you to come back."

Shrugging, I laughed uneasily and said, "It must've worked. I don't
know why else I'd come here."

Jenni followed me to the kitchen of the annex building, announcing my entry while Marcus's mother prepared me a plate of salad and spaghetti. "Alright, so I came back," I said to Con Underwood while eating. "I didn't mean to give anybody a heart attack."

"It's just that we're glad to see you."

Checking his face to see if his lip had curled in sarcasm, I crammed a forkful of salad in my mouth and said, "Yeah, give me some of that church talk."

"No, really, I'm glad you're here. I wish you could have been here this afternoon. We had a great time."

"What did you do?"

"Nothing all that much. I mean, we played touch football. Nothing serious. The guys and the girls together. Just having fun."

I resisted the temptation to suggest something lewd.

"And we showed them the town."

"That killed a good five minutes."

"We took them to the mill and by the school and to the track. Imagine us showing these people from Atlanta our track. But they seemed genuinely impressed. It was fun, but the best time for me was after we'd been to the Humdinger and were riding around awhile and we just stopped the cars on the side of the road and walked out in the middle of a field and lay down in the grass and talked."

Flashing across my mind came images of a Saturday afternoon more than a year earlier, of Marcus parking his Mustang on the side of a new road near his house, of Andrew and me watching him curiously as he stared across a field at a ridge between two patches of woods. "They're putting a house up there," he said. "I can't believe it. When we were kids we used to play army up on that hill all day long. Our parents would have to hunt us down for supper, and we didn't want to go home then. Not a care in the world," he said, his voice curiously choking. He opened the door to the Mustang and said, "You're going to think I've gone insane, but I've got to do this." He started running up the hill, raking its crest with imaginary machine-gun fire. Laughing, Andrew and I followed, pulling the pins from imaginary grenades, diving to the ground as we whistled the approach of incoming bombs. Each of us took multiple hits but continued limping toward the top of the hill until Andrew screamed in genuine pain. "Hold it. Hold it," he yelled, clutching at his finger before putting it to his lips. "I've caught a briar."

Marcus dropped to his knees laughing. "The entire Nazi army can't stop him, but he's put out of commission by a briar." We lay on the crest of the hill laughing until exhausted and silent, almost dozing, for how long I didn't know, more than likely only a few minutes, but perhaps hours, time playing tricks, for at that moment something happened for the first time in five or six years: the courthouse clock struck the hour. I lay with eyes shut hoping that maybe by some act of God I had slipped back to an easier time and would return home tonight to find George in his recliner, Daddy entering the door, smiling and apologizing for being late, and I could tell them how confused everything had become while they were gone and how glad I was to have them back. Marcus had broken the spell by saying that someone had fixed the courthouse clock and if it really was four o'clock we'd best go home and get ready for the evening's basketball game. But I had always remembered that moment, the intense longing for a chance to go back, to start over, to not allow myself to be so trapped by the manipulations of others. I'd be my own person.

"We just talked, about life, about how we felt about things," Con was saying, his voice turning apologetic as he said, "About God. I know it sounds crazy."

"No, I don't think it sounds crazy," I muttered to Con. And to no one in particular I muttered, "Not at all." I felt strangely sober, as if I had suddenly awakened from a long stupor of denying everything that had taken place around me. Since the bomb had exploded I had tried every means of escape, alcohol, sports, even a thwarted attempt to run away, but nothing had improved. I hated being alive as much as ever. Something had to be more important than playing ball. Hadn't my father said it, "You just wake up one day, son, and realize there are more important things in life than playing ball." And certainly more important than getting drunk, more important than hunting for pleasure. But what was it? Morose, I withdrew in silence as around me the teenagers chattered. Something was happening to me. Some strange new thought was trying to enter my brain.

Later that night the group met in the tiny fellowship hall where years ago we once had sung as children and where now someone had erected a cross fashioned from a small pine tree, its rough bark still intact, an ugly encroachment upon the beauty of a church familiar only with engraved crosses of polished brass smudged not by blood, but by fingerprints, artificial and sterile emblems unlike the starkly real one before me. "A hell of a way to die," I thought, staring at the tree. "Nailed up like that." And suddenly a thought I had never before considered struck me clearly, like a sword piercing my heart: It was real. As real as my own father's murder. An ashen corpse splattered with blood with loved ones viewing from outside the cordons. Why should it be hard to believe that it really happened?

I became aware that flitting through my mind was a tune I'd often sung as a child in this same room, "He died on the cross to save us from sin. Everybody ought to love Jesus."

"Yes," I thought. "Everybody ought to. I ought to." And with that thought came the sensation of a presence in the room hovering over me; did others sense it, too? I glanced toward Jim and his girlfriend, toward Con and Peggy Jean and Truckie Myers, clinging to his girlfriend's arm. Did they feel the presence? What if they didn't? What if they thought I was crazy? No, what they thought no longer mattered. I would do what I knew was right. Baxter was talking. What about I wasn't sure. But after he finally ended by saying, "If anyone has anything to say to the group, we want you to have the chance now," I stood up and said, "Well, I've got something to say."

Chapter
Twenty-seven

The moment was so profound that I have wrestled with it ever since. At times I've wondered why I never again experienced such an overwhelming presence, at other times have thought that perhaps I now feel it more often than not, that it's the first kiss that fills us with the most sensation and that subsequent kisses, though wonderful, can be as taken for granted as a drink of water. Such a moment leaves people grappling for words, like Augustine, who said, "there was infused in my heart something like the light of full certainty," or John Wesley, who said, "I felt my heart strangely warmed," language that can evoke images of indigestion or electric charges, evoking chuckles from us until we try to put such an experience into words ourselves.

All I knew was that the next morning I felt more alive than I ever had. Had those robins been singing outside my window every morning this spring? Had the sun always risen with such beauty to warm a May morning? The smell of bacon drifted from the kitchen, and lying still, I could hear the grease popping and Mama stirring in the hall and Freddy snoring in the bunk bed, and I felt a burst of energy foreign to my mornings.

"I've changed," I told Reverend Berry as I stood on the roots of a big oak after the worship service. "My life is going to be different."

"You've had a spiritual awakening," he said. "And it's real. And I'm glad this has happened for you. But you won't always feel this way."

No, I thought. He was wrong. I would always feel this way.

"But why would it wear off?"

"Trust me. Not everybody will understand what you're telling me. Not even people in this church. But I believe that what you have experienced is real. And I'm glad you told me about this," he said. "God has really touched you. He can use you to touch others."

Someone to touch immediately came to mind. I wanted to tell Elana Rosemont. After lunch I phoned her. Mr. Rosemont answered and called her to the phone. She took her time before answering.

"Elana," I said. "This is Dickey."

"Yes, I know," she said, her voice unsteady.

"Listen, Elana. I've got something to tell you."

She was silent.

"It's something good, Elana."

"Yes?" Her voice changed. She sounded curious.

"I've been to church this weekend."

"You, Dickey?" she asked. "You went to church? I mean—I'm glad you went to church. I just got back myself." She seemed more at ease now.

"Elana, I don't know how to say this, but I know God was there. That sounds funny, I know, I mean He's supposed to be there at church, but—I mean, He was really there."

"No, that doesn't sound funny."

"You know what I'm talking about?"

"I think so."

"Isn't it great?"

She laughed and said, "Well, yes it is. I mean, it really is."

"This has made me feel different about some things, Elana. A lot of things. I want to apologize for what I said to you last weekend."

She was silent, and for a moment I was afraid she thought I was teasing her or making up a blasphemous lie. "Elana," I said. "I'm more serious than I've ever been in my life. And I am sorry. Please forgive me."

Then I heard a sniffle. And what sounded like a sob, or was it laughter? "Elana?"

"I forgive you, Dickey."

I sighed and said, "Thank you."

She laughed pleasantly, prompting me to smile and draw upon some courage to say words perhaps I'd spoken sometime in my childhood, though I couldn't remember when, and even now felt I must prepare her for them. "I want you know something and I hope you understand what I mean."

"Yeah?"

"I love you, Elana. I mean, I really do love you."

"I understand," she said, before saying something I never thought I'd hear. "Dickey, I love you, too."

Chapter
Twenty-eight

Elana Rosemont and I never went out on a date. She graduated three weeks later, soon left for college, and I never saw her much any more. But I was too busy to mourn for long; suddenly I found myself popular with girls who pinned the reputation of "nice guy, like a big brother" on me. I was elected not only president of the senior class but also president of the United Methodist Youth. Our football team won nine games, our basketball team twenty, before losing in the semi-finals of the state tournament.

Every week of my senior year had brought its challenges and victories, and during the excitement it was easy somehow to forget ever being a freshman beaten around at practice by seniors, or watching games from the bench, easy to believe the successes came because God was showing favoritism and that never again would frustration return.

But the fairy tale ended after graduation, when the applause died and the attempts to play college basketball and baseball ended during my junior year at the university, when I woke up one morning and realized there were more important things in life than playing ball and began to take more seriously my studies in journalism.

Had I not taken seriously an assignment in a composition class I probably never would have had the idea to visit the old man in the hospital. But there I'd been, struggling with the assignment, interview and write about someone who has affected your life, when Peggy

Jean phoned: "Some kind of hernia operation," she said. "He might die." And then she added wistfully, "I wish he would."

Listening to the voice of impulse I found myself within twenty minutes of her call walking through the door of the hospital, my pulse increasing as I stopped at a desk where two women dressed in peppermint-colored dresses sat. "May I help you?" asked one woman.

I cleared my throat and said, "I wanted to visit a patient here."

"What's the name?"

"Mister A. C. Park."

"Let's see," she mumbled, turning the pages of a notebook. "Park. Park. No, I don't see it . . ."

"Maybe it's listed under Cliff Park."

"No, I don't see him," she said. "We don't have a Park—oh, wait, he's on the fourth floor," and before she could finish speaking, I thanked her and hustled through the lobby and toward the public elevator, turning the corner to see Peggy Jean walking down the corridor. I pushed the button, hoping the elevator door would open before I had to acknowledge her, but the door stayed shut and she accosted me. "What are you doing here?"

"Oh, uh, I just had to come—uh—visit somebody who's sick."

"Who do you know over here who's sick? One of your friends in here?"

"Yeah."

"Who is it?"

"You wouldn't know him," I said, thinking better of giving her a false name, not with notebooks and women in peppermint dresses able to dispute my lies.

"Dickey," she said, her eyes lighting with recognition. "You can't go up there and see him."

"Why not?"

"For one thing, he's on the fourth floor and I doubt if they even let his family up there to see him. And anyway, what do you think Mama would say if she knew? She'd die."

"I'm not planning on telling Mama."

"You're liable to get arrested for going up there. They probably have armed guards. You don't know what you're doing."

"Maybe I don't, but I've got to try."

"Why?"

"I don't know," I said as the door opened and I entered the elevator, lacking the words to sort out what I'd come to question: that if God were ever going to intervene in the world, and put a stop to insults and lies and bomb murders and the hatred in the hearts of survivors, would He do so by reaching his own hand down from the sky or by prompting survivors to reach with their own hands from across the room? Would I spend the rest of my life with emotions controlled by another? Or would I take charge of my life, even if no one understood why I was doing it, and release my hatred for a human being who, like myself on many occasions, pulled by the manipulations of others, had done what maybe he thought himself incapable of doing. It was easy and permissible to hate anyone that you feared. But I would not fear Cliff Park. And with God's help neither would I hate him. And so I would face him.

"It's just something I've got to do." I said.

The door closed and I pushed the button, my heart pounding. I took two deep breaths before I reached the fourth floor and walked down the hallway to a counter where two nurses with puzzled stares watched my approach. "Could you tell me which way to Cliff Park's room?"

"Are you family?"

"Close," I said, meeting her gaze and smiling.

She hesitated before answering. "First door on your left." I walked toward the room, wondering where the guards were stationed and when they would suddenly pounce on me and search for the gun I could have smuggled into the room to shoot the old man.

The door was ajar. I took a deep breath, annoyed at the trembling of my hands. Why, I really was scared of him. I took another deep breath and knocked lightly, pushing open the door.

He was alone. He sat in a chair and stared at the wall beneath the television, his skin yellow beneath the white hospital gown. With his tongue he clicked his bottom false teeth out of place, and for a moment, the image came to mind of him at his trial, listening to the evidence mounting against him, playing to the audience, confident and smiling. In the courtroom he had seemed confident and tall. In this hospital room, he appeared small and frail and yellow. He worked his teeth and did not turn toward me until after I'd said softly, my voice breaking, "Mister Park." He sized me up with a stern gaze.

"Mister Park," I said, walking toward him, "I'm—now I don't want to upset you or anything, but I'm kin to Mister Hoard."

His stare was upon me now, his face revealing no trace of interest, as if he failed to recognize the name. "I'm down here at the university now," I stammered, "studying journalism. And thought maybe I could interview you and write a paper for class. I thought maybe you could tell me something about the day my—Mister Hoard was killed. When did you hear about his death? How did you hear? Radio, maybe? What were you doing when you heard about it?"

His expression never changed, his unblinking eyes like the eyes of a dead man, his mouth working his bottom teeth.

"Now," I said. "I'm not trying to pull any information out of you. I just wanted to find out what you were doing."

He broke the interminable silence that followed by finally saying, "I don't believe I have nothing to say to you."

"Fine," I said, setting down my legal pad and pen. "That's fine. We don't have to talk about that. I—I just thought maybe you would. I heard you'd been sick and just thought I'd—well, what exactly has been wrong?"

Several seconds of painful silence was broken when he glanced down at his swollen belly and said, "I had the hernias. I had an operation for the hernias."

"That—I guess—must be pretty rough."

He looked back toward the wall and said, "Yep, it's been pretty rough."

"Well," I said uncomfortably, not really knowing what to say, opting for "You seem to be getting along better. I mean, I guess you're doing better."

"Yeah, I'm some better," he said.

"Well, that's good," I said. "That's good. Uh, do you have many visitors?"

"No, not too many. My wife come to see me today, and my daughter's been by. But that's about it."

"I know you were glad to see them."

"Yeah," he said. "It means a lot. Family means a lot."

"I guess they're relieved you're doing better."

"Yes, they've been real worried. This almost got me, though. It almost got me."

Uneasily, I said, "But it didn't. You're still here." After another long silence, I said, "Well, I guess I'll let you rest." I was breathing deeper now, no longer afraid of him. Why, take him away from his cronies, remove his audience, and he was just an old man facing the inevitable. The "hernias" hadn't got him. But something else would. It just wasn't going to be me. I no longer wanted to be the one to kill him. For I, too, knew something about conspiracies, and about hurting others to either look big or to save face. And this old man needed forgiveness every bit as much as I.

He had clicked the lower teeth from his mouth and left them over his lip. I reached out my hand. He took it and I said, "Goodbye." He did not acknowledge my departure as I walked to the door but when I turned and said, "Mister Park," he flinched, his eyes widening when he saw my raised elbow and extended arm, and it occurred to me that maybe he had expected to find aimed between his eyes not my finger, but a gun. He had been every bit as afraid of me as I of him. And for good reason. I could have walked in that room and blown his head off. He stared at my hand, curious now. I smiled and straightened up my shoulders. "Mister Park," I said, raising my finger and pointing toward the ceiling. "Somebody up there still loves you."

He said nothing, turning again toward the wall, clicking his teeth, staring at nothing. I closed the door behind me and walked down the hall, a free man.